*Living
a Charmed Life*

Books by Victoria Moran

Creating a Charmed Life:
Sensible, Spiritual Secrets Every Busy Woman Should Know

Fat, Broke & Lonely No More:
Your Personal Solution to Overeating,
Overspending, and Looking for Love
in All the Wrong Places

Fit from Within:
101 Simple Secrets to Change Your Body and Your Life

Lit from Within:
A Simple Guide to the Art of Inner Beauty

The Love-Powered Diet:
Eating for Freedom, Health, and Joy

Shelter for the Spirit:
Create Your Own Haven in a Hectic World

Younger by the Day:
365 Ways to Rejuvenate Your Body and Revitalize Your Spirit

Living
a Charmed Life

YOUR GUIDE TO FINDING MAGIC
IN EVERY MOMENT OF EVERY DAY

Victoria Moran

HarperOne
An Imprint of HarperCollins*Publishers*

HarperOne

HarperCollins books may be purchased for educational, business, or sales promotional use. For information please write: Special Markets Department, HarperCollins Publishers, 10 East 53rd Street, New York, NY 10022.

Grateful acknowledgment is given for excerpted material used in the book. For complete listings, please see page 247, which constitutes as a continuation of this copyright page.

HarperCollins Web site: http://www.harpercollins.com

HarperCollins®, ☰®, and HarperOne™ are trademarks of HarperCollins Publishers

Designed by Sharon VanLoozenoord

FIRST HARPERCOLLINS PAPERBACK EDITION PUBLISHED IN 2010

Library of Congress Cataloging-in-Publication Data

Moran, Victoria.
  Living a charmed life : your guide to finding magic in every moment of every day / Victoria Moran. — 1st ed.
      p. cm.
  ISBN 978−0−06−164990−5
  1. Women—Conduct of life.
  2. Self-actualization (Psychology) I. Title.
  BJ1610.M652 2009
  158.1—dc22
                                        2008051466

10 11 12 13 14 CW 10 9 8 7 6 5 4 3 2 1

Contents

Introduction ix

1 Know that you are worthy 1

2 Start a serendipity log 5

3 Enlist your inner epicure 9

4 . . . And your inner chaperone 13

5 Wake up and smell the morning 17

6 Expect the best 21

7 Give something away today 25

8 Behold the thousand-pound gorilla 29

9 Admire all your aspects 33

10 Make life-charming decisions 37

11 Bring back chivalry 41

12 Wash the dishes with all your heart 45

13 Dress for the occasion 49

14 Slow down 55

15 Stay close to what makes you come alive 59

16 Become surprisingly fit 63

17 Seek out your life stories 67

18 Live richly 71

19 Prioritize the people who matter 77

20 . . . Then connect with the rest of us 81

21 . . . And sometimes savor solitude 85

22 Add a splash of red 89

23 Grow green gracefully 93

24 Keep your sunny side up 97

25 Take such good care of yourself 101

26   *Ease the e-mail onslaught* 105

27   *Put fear in its place* 111

28   *Not guilty, Your Honor* 117

29   *Write yourself a life list* 121

30   *Detox your body* 125

31   *Detox your life* 133

32   *Fill your life with beauty* 139

33   *Do the cosmic two-step* 143

34   *Indulge in your simplest pleasure* 147

35   *Take train trips and road trips* 151

36   *Claim a cafe* 155

37   *Be completely, utterly yourself* 157

38   *Map the route from bummed to better* 163

39   *Give peace a chance* 167

40   *Consider yourself lucky* 173

41   *Gather the gurus* 177

42   *Prepare for your future* 183

43   *Don't overlook the obvious* 187

44   *Make something* 193

45   *Enliven your diet* 197

46   *KC, here I come* 203

47   *Proceed despite detractors* 209

48   *Re-create a charmed life if you have to* 215

49   *Love it. Then maybe leave it.* 219

50   *Be the one to prove this stuff* 225

     Resources for a Charmed Life 229

     Permissions 247

     Acknowledgments 249

     About the Author 251

Introduction

Just over ten years ago, I was given the go-ahead to write a book called *Creating a Charmed Life: Sensible, Spiritual Secrets Every Busy Woman Should Know.* It proposed that living in shades of gray is unnecessary when Technicolor is an option. That book's mission was to help women apply elementary spiritual principles to everyday life and as a result discover beauty in the ordinary and wonder in simple things. It apparently did its job, because it became a word-of-mouth bestseller, translated into twenty-eight languages and still very much alive as one woman after another discovers it and gives copies as gifts to her sisters, daughters, and friends.

Living a Charmed Life is a similarly structured collection of action-inspiring essays. It is in one sense a tenth-anniversary sequel, bringing full circle the process of custom-crafting a remarkable life. And yet this book is very much its own, coming from (and responding to) a different point in time. It invites you to discover the magical elements in every nanosecond of your time on earth, when they're obvious and when they're not.

Living a Charmed Life comes with a context. When I wrote its predecessor, I found myself in the midst of creative chaos. I was newly married to my second husband, William, after living as a young widow and single mom for several years. We were rehabbing an antique house. Homeschooling (and chauffeuring) my daughter, Adair, a budding actress then fourteen, took lots of time and gave me even more joy. (Adair was "Rachael" in *Creating a Charmed Life,* but shortly after its publication she started going by her middle name.) At this same time, I was learning to be a stepmom to William's children, who were with us part of the time. His daughter, Siân, was an artistic eleven-year-old who loved to read. Erik, nine, was, like his dad, quiet and conscientious. Six-year-old James was bright, curious, and determined to keep up with the older kids.

My freshly blended life wasn't easy, but it was fully, richly, and constantly engaging. Out of that time of sensory overload and of novel experiences coming at me like collapsing dominos, I wrote about forming a bliss-kissed life from the good wet clay of busyness and energy.

I needed another decade, however, to learn how to stay in touch with the magical nature of things in light of events that transpired in my own life and those that took place in the larger world and have affected us all. In one *Creating a Charmed Life* essay entitled "Invite Adventure," I referred to modern life as "sleepily safe." That's not a phrase anyone would use to describe things today. Even the most self-contained among us have been called to respond to the political, economic, and environmental distresses of this moment in time. As the realities that make up the background of our lives continue to readjust and redesign themselves, the act of creating a dazzling life calls for more courage, inventiveness, and flexibility than it once did. We have the daunting charge of taking into account, in our every dealing, all the other beings to whom we're connected and the future of a planet. Even when we're not consciously thinking of that big picture, a part of us always knows it's there.

Nevertheless, we do most of our living privately and close to home. In that personal portion of my own life, I have learned in these ten years that even fulfilled dreams require skillful maintenance.

Hanging out on earth is messy under any circumstances: you can take all the organizing classes in the adult-ed catalog and there will still be loose ends, the uncontrollable, the inexplicable. And sometimes something really awful happens.

A week after my publisher commissioned the book you're holding, my stepson James, just sixteen, died suddenly from a virus that attacked his pancreas. There was no warning, only a call to William's mobile phone as we waited to board a flight at LAX. In a split second, everything changed. Meeting each day, facing the loss, and supporting my husband in his deep, deep grief took precedence over writing a book. We decided to simplify things by moving out of my beloved New York City, a decision that proved, for me, to be another cause for sorrow. When I finally sat down to write during that snow-covered winter in a strange place, I was met with a hard question: how could I write about living a charmed life when tragedies, both old and new, had left shards of sadness that could not be wished away?

I told a friend what I was wrestling with. He said, "Think about it this way: what do you see that you do for other people?" I felt that I'd been put on the spot, like I was supposed to come up with some fancy corporate mission statement. "I don't know," I said, "I think I help them remember the magic." And he said, "Precisely. That's all you need to do." I knew in that instant that he was right. Losses and detours and disappointments—most fleeting, but some profound—are a part of every life. In a charmed one, however, beauty and joy and wonder and serendipity are every bit as real and obvious. We have the option of living in their light, regardless of what else we're going through.

The secret is to remember this, although we're most apt to forget it when we need it most (and I emphatically include myself in that *we*). When I become amnesic and am momentarily lost in despair, someone needs to remind me to tap into my spiritual connection, a source of unending strength and inspiration when I think to call on it; and then to get up and do something: to put into play practical, workable techniques for opening my personal life to what a mentor of mine used to call "the upward progression of the universe." I've written this book to be that reminder for you.

In it you'll find fifty chapter-essays designed to help you live a remarkable life, however you define *remarkable*. Each chapter closes with what I call a "lucky charm," a specific action you can take to apply the essence of that essay—immediately, in many cases. The essays are in sequential order, and a few times you'll find a couple that play off each other (e.g., "Enlist Your Inner Epicure" followed by ". . . And Your Inner Chaperone"). Therefore, I recommend that you read *Living a Charmed Life* all the way through the first time. After that, if you want to keep it on your nightstand or toss it into your gym bag and read a chapter you're drawn to, or simply one you come to when you open the book at random, that works, too.

There are essays here that cover overarching topics, like upping your optimism and mitigating such negative states of mind as fear and guilt. Some are pure practicality. ("Live Richly" has to do with financial well-being; "Ease the E-mail Onslaught" needs no further explanation.) Others, including "Take Train Trips and Road Trips" and "Add a Splash of Red," deal with the charmed-life necessities of lightness and fun. And because you can't go off on a charmed-life adventure without your body coming along, you'll get tips on caring for your physical self in "Become Surprisingly Fit," "Detox Your Body," and "Enliven Your Diet."

At the heart of living a charmed life, however, is the spiritual dimension. Key essays such as "Stay Close to What Makes You Come Alive," "Do the Cosmic Two-Step," and "Give Peace a Chance" pertain to your inner life, your spiritual self. Because everyone comes from a unique point of view on such matters and we use different words to express ourselves in this arena, I invite you to do a "quick translation" if something I've written doesn't sit quite right with your spiritual sensibilities. I take a very eclectic view and draw inspiration from many religious and philosophical traditions. Take what works for you and leave the rest. I'm honored that you're allowing me to be your guide for a time, but your charmed life is *your* charmed life. It develops within the context of your worldview.

On a more mundane level: a bibliography! At the back of this book, you'll find "Resources for a Charmed Life," a combination of explanatory notes and recommendations of books, Web sites, and even a few "field trip" destinations. I've made a point of keeping this resource section as readable as the book itself so you'll want to delve into it.

Finally, I feel the need to add a note on gender. The vast majority of my readers are women, and this book's predecessor even noted in its subtitle that it was for a female audience. I've followed up with the same assumption here. However, I am aware that some men do read my books. I welcome you—feminine default pronouns notwithstanding—and hope you'll find something useful here.

And to every reader, as you start or continue your charmed-life adventure, I wish you all good things. It is my sincere belief that an enchanted way of being is available to anyone, during good times and bad. It asks only that your connection to the wisdom inside you stay strong and certain, and that you be willing to take action on the days you feel like it and on the days you don't. As you follow this path, you'll come to notice fortunate coincidences, exquisite inter-ludes, and fulfilled hopes sprouting up across the landscape of your life like wildflowers in a spring meadow. The more you recognize and appreciate them, the more of them you'll have to recognize and appreciate. ❀

Living
a Charmed Life

1

Know that you are worthy

Nothing you have done, nothing that was done
to you, and nothing anyone else has ever said to
you or believed about you erases the inalienable
truth that you are one delectable creation.

Most of us waste a lot of time distrusting ourselves and discounting
ourselves. As hard as we work to instill confidence in our children,
it can be difficult to maintain healthy self-esteem ourselves. We
might feel very competent about certain talents and aptitudes; we
could even feel smug and superior in some aspects of life. Despite in-
termittent bravado, however, underneath there is often the shadow
thought "If they only knew the truth, they'd be disappointed."

It's up to you to know the truth, the real truth about yourself.
That is: *you are an expression of the beneficence that brought you
forth*. Of course you have more to learn as you go along, and you've
done things in the past that you wish you hadn't. A valid definition
of *human being* might be: "intelligent biped who has more to learn
and who has done things he/she wishes that he/she hadn't." This is
who you are in your current model—that is, Homo sapiens living

on earth. You're no more unworthy because of that fact than a bicycle is unworthy because it isn't a spaceship.

Personally, I thought I had the self-worth thing down pretty well. I mean, I've worked on myself for a long time, and as a certified life coach I help other people realize that they are fully worthy of getting to where they want to be. That's why what happened at Cafe Gratitude, a vegan restaurant in San Rafael, California, was such a big deal for me. The name of every item on the menu there—appetizers, entrées, desserts, drinks—is an affirmation. If you were ordering several courses, you'd say to the server when you gave your order: "I am grateful, I am joyful, I am brilliant, and I am beautiful." When she served each dish, instead of saying, "Your spinach salad," she would say, "You are grateful" (or "joyful" or "brilliant" or whatever it is).

I was there with my friend Julie, and because we were catching up for the first time in a couple of years, I didn't pay too much attention to what I ordered. When the young server brought me the dish, however, she said, "You are worthy." I was taken aback. People have told me a lot of nice things in my life, but this was the first time anyone ever looked me in the eye and said, "You are worthy."

It is embarrassing to tell you (after authoring ten self-help books) that my life was changed by one line from an abundantly pierced and tattooed twenty-three-year-old, but it was. When she said, "You are worthy," I had to get over confusing my human failings with my basic value. It seemed at the time that I had to either accept my worth once and for all, or send my quinoa and tofu back to the kitchen.

I hope that you can go to California and dine at Cafe Gratitude. Until then, serve yourself a generous portion of self-worth every day—and rename what's for dinner!

This is useful as a way to make up for what more than likely happened in your early life, even if you came from a loving home. The standard scenario goes like this: We debut as babies, perfect and full of ourselves, but over time even that expression—"full of yourself"—takes on a negative connotation. The surety of our divine heritage and limitless value, which we knew so well in our earliest years, erodes as we're told what not to touch and what not to say, or when we're even once given a label like "chubby" or "slow" or "troublemaker." Some of us had religious training that, well meaning though it may have been, focused so much on sin that some innermost part of ourselves never made it to redemption. In school we got grades, and many of us are still grading ourselves on every aspect of our being.

It is time to outgrow self-doubt. You are worthy. Nothing you have done, nothing that was done to you, and nothing anyone else has ever said to you or believed about you erases the inalienable truth that you are one delectable creation. Always were, always will be. You are worthy. Eat your tofu.

Lucky Charm

*Choose a common action (like looking in a mirror
or walking through a door), and every time you
do it, remind yourself that you are worthy.*

2

Start a serendipity log

Preventive medicine
for charmed-life blackouts
is to keep a serendipity log,
an ongoing list of wonders, delights,
and positive coincidences.

It's a pity when someone is living a charmed life but doesn't know it. This can happen when ambition gets out of whack ("I'm only in a TV series when I ought to be in feature films") or when a person is too busy to recognize the boons and blessings that appear every day. Preventive medicine for charmed-life blackouts is to keep a serendipity log, an ongoing list of the wonders, delights, and positive coincidences that appear as answered prayers or those unbidden perks life presents just because the Light (God, Spirit, Universe— pick your name) is trying to speak to you all the time.

To get started, put a little notebook in your purse. You'll find that it has multiple uses: jotting down snippets of inspiration, staying on top of the day's activities, keeping track of the money you

spend, *and* making note of the serendipities showering you throughout the day. These are little joys such as:

> "A co-worker gave me a copy of the novel that I can't get
> from the library for another six weeks."
>
> "I just found out that I'm going to be in Cincinnati the same
> weekend as my friend from Seattle."
>
> "I not only got the single available parking spot, but an SUV
> had been there and left so much space that parallel park-
> ing was a breeze."
>
> "After looking for weeks for the right paint color, I saw it
> on the wall at Pottery Barn and the salesclerk knew
> the name of it."

6

Most of the time, our serendipities come as normal events like
these. When you're aware of them, you start to see that every day
is filled with little boosts. They keep you going when you haven't
had a jackpot-sized windfall for far too long. It was like that when
my ever-gracious literary agent, Linda Chester, gave me a bottle of
fine champagne. I put it away to save until something extraordinary happened. Months passed. I wondered when there would be a
reason to pop that cork.

A year went by, then a second. Whenever I saw the golden box
with the champagne inside, I felt sorry for myself, thinking that I'd
had this accoutrement to celebration for so long but nothing particularly celebratory had taken place. That's when I knew that I
needed a serendipity log. In waiting so intently for my proverbial
ship to come in, I'd been missing the beautiful sailboats and pleasure crafts that were part of my life all the time.

So I got out a pen and wrote:

"I have a fabulous bottle of champagne and I can use it
    to toast anything I like, anytime I want."
"I showed up at the box office at 8:02 without a reservation
    and got a 5th row center seat for *Gypsy*."
"My husband commented this morning that I needed a
    covered tumbler for taking my juice to the gym,
    and this afternoon I was invited to a Tupperware
    party."

Noticing (and noting) such events as these is like giving a house-plant a shot of fertilizer. The plant responds to the latter; life responds to the former. I don't pretend to know how it all works, but in my imagination I think of heavenly beings assigned to the Serendipity Department. It's a massive job, because every serendipitous event requires separate lives and seemingly unrelated events to intersect for the benefit of all concerned. (Chaos theorists must detest serendipity.) In any case, when I am aware of this exquisite orchestration, and grateful for it, it's as if those angelic forces get wind of the fact and figure out how to send more goodness my way. You may have noticed this in your life, too, and if you keep a serendipity log, you surely will notice it.

As you go about your business paying attention to each joy you come upon, every now and then life will present you with a Really Big Deal. Nearly three years after that champagne took up residence in my wine cellar (OK, that place under the kitchen sink where there's enough room for a bottle to lie sideways), and I'd been doing the serendipity log for a while, it happened.

7

I'd wanted an apartment of our own in New York City for so long it was starting to feel like the quixotic "impossible dream." Buying a place the size we needed for kids' visits and two offices as well as regular life had always seemed just beyond our means. I'd all but given up on either Manhattan or Brooklyn until the morning I saw online a Harlem condominium that had, at a manageable price, everything I'd held in my vision—light, space, location—and astounding perks: a gym, "green construction," even music-practice rooms for William. (He plays the accordion. He needs a soundproof room.)

We moved in on a sunny October day and toasted our new home with that champagne. My serendipity log read: "Miracle! We really live here. We drank the champagne." It also says: "I walked Aspen and Oliver" (my daughter's adorable dogs); "My sunblock was in the first box I unpacked—no searching"; and "I discovered a juice bar in the neighborhood."

This is key: appreciating *all* serendipities. There is a time for champagne, and a time for carrot juice. There are times for weddings and births and big trips, for new jobs and promotions and dream homes. And there are times for putting on sunblock and walking the dogs. When you can see all such events as serendipitous proof that you are cherished beyond comprehension, you'll live a charmed life. And know it. And own it.

Lucky Charm
☘

Put a cute little notebook in your bag,
and write down the serendipities that grace
your life every day.

8

3

Enlist your inner epicure

The only time your inner epicure will get out of
hand and start pillaging chocolate shops and
picking up traveling salesmen is when you deny
her until she just can't take it anymore.

Pleasure is good for you. Where you can run into trouble is looking for pleasure that isn't worthy of you. Accepting junk, whether
in the form of merchandise, food, or relationships, does not—
cannot—provide us with genuine pleasure. As a result, we often go
for more junk and end up disliking ourselves because we look over
our lives and don't see the quality we long for.

There's happy news: your rescuer is at hand. She resides inside you, in fact, in the form of your *inner epicure.* This is the part
of you that delights in the pleasures of being alive: fine food and
drink, romance, friendship, travel—the assorted sensory and intel-
lectual delights that are yours to sample because you had the nerve
to show up on this demanding planet and star in your own life.

It's common to keep the inner epicure hidden away. We're
afraid that she's a glutton, a trollop, and a dilettante, some shameful

aspect of ourselves that is endlessly greedy and self-absorbed. Not true. She's the part of you that enables you to enjoy your very own life. It probably is more blessed to give than receive, but this particular aspect of your personality is here to help you relish the receiving piece. The only time she'll get out of hand and start pillaging chocolate shops and picking up traveling salesmen is when you deny her until she just can't take it anymore.

You call on her by developing a healthy respect for pleasure and doing what you can to get all you need. She's there when you take the time to savor delicious meals, wear clothing that feels smooth and soothing next to your skin, and sleep on a comfortable bed with a heavenly pillow or a pile of them. She's happy when you laugh enough and love enough. She cheers when you allow your body to have needs and you're not embarrassed about meeting them. She's packed and ready to roll when you set out to sample new delights, refining your preferences and expanding your scope as you do.

When you're on board with your inner epicure, you take great care of your physical self, but you're never one of those women who "don't eat" or who, if they do, say something ridiculous like, "I'm being so *bad*." You give your sex life time and attention. If it's not as scrumptious as it ought to be, you find ways to spice it up. You allocate some of your budget for movies and theater and massages—or whatever makes you feel that you're not just working to stay afloat, but reveling in the voyage.

You strengthen this partnership by remembering that you are a grown-up. You're well aware of what you like. You need no one's permission to meet your needs and experience whatever physical, mental, or spiritual deliciousness appeals to you right now. Other than in extraordinary circumstances (e.g., you're on a special diet for a health condition and not yet sure of its various permutations), you don't have to check out your choices with someone who knows more. Who could possibly know more about what makes you happy than you?

Your inner epicure has certain standards. She isn't fond of settling, but if extenuating circumstances make this necessary, she'll help you settle with style. Dinner may be rice and beans, but you can serve it on your mother's china, set the table with old silver, and snip some lilacs from the garden as a centerpiece.

The pleasure seeker inside you is keenly aware that this is her shot. *You* are an eternal being. You've been around forever and you'll last as long as the heavens. Your inner epicure, however, is part of your physical life, *this* physical life. She doesn't have forever, and she puts great stock in the moment at hand. Let her come out to play. She'll lead you to the tastiest strawberries, the prettiest dresses, and the most scrumptious love affairs, even if you have those liaisons all with one person.

When she gets her due, your inner epicure is a great friend of your health and happiness. She has no interest in overdoing, and she doesn't want you harmed even a little bit. Why would she? You're the only way she gets to eat the strawberries and wear the dresses. Listen: she's talking to you, telling you to live a little. Do it. You'll both be a great deal happier.

Lucky Charm

Do something intensely gratifying within the next twenty-four hours. And after you do, have no regrets.

... And your inner chaperone

Your inner chaperone
helps you live successfully by showing you
where "peak experience" stops
and "downhill from here" begins.

Your inner epicure is there to ensure that you'll enjoy the pleasures of life to the fullest. You also have an *inner chaperone*. Her job is to help you put the stops on, to say no to what will not serve your ultimate health, happiness, and success.

It is a curious thing that many of us seek to help ourselves by harming ourselves. If something goes wrong or we're having an off day, we might seek comfort in the wrong food or the wrong man. Convinced that we deserve some down time, we might put off doing what needs to be done, assuming that next weekend we'll actually *want* to work on our taxes or dig into the clutter pile. We may "treat ourselves" to a new outfit or electronic toy without the cash to pay for it. We put it on a charge card, oblivious to the fact that, without some shifting or saving, we won't have any more money to spare the day the bill comes due than we have now.

When we feel tired or afraid, or when we've been hurt or we get down on ourselves, we develop mental myopia: the only thing that matters is this instant and patching up the discomfort with some distraction. What that distraction will cost us later—whether in discomfort, self-recrimination, or interest charges—is the furthest thought from our minds. This is where the inner chaperone comes in, providing guidance on how to genuinely care for ourselves—body, spirit, self-esteem, and bank account.

Foresight is your inner chaperone's forte. She knows how much you would enjoy a night out (your inner epicure is her little sister, after all), and she knows how much more you'll enjoy it if you eat judiciously, drink moderately, spend rationally, and don't do anything you would come to regret. You might think of her as the fairy godmother in the Disney version of *Cinderella*. She's not a tyrant or an uptight killjoy at all, and it really is in your own best interest that she wants you home by midnight. Your inner chaperone is invested in your living successfully. She helps by showing you where "peak experience" stops and "downhill from here" begins. Her wisdom is inside you right now if you'll listen and follow it.

6 Tips Your Inner Chaperone Might Give You

1. *Understand, my dear, that moderation is not deprivation.* "Enough is a banquet," somebody told me once. (Maybe it was my inner chaperone.)

2. *Give yourself gentle parameters, and practice staying within them.* If you decide to be in bed by 10 p.m., TiVo the show you want to watch, no matter how eager you are to see what happens. If you've told yourself that you'll work on

your novel or your memoir an hour a day, that means an hour today, not some hypothetical day that may never come.

3. Practice stopping just before you want to. In the buffet line or at the outlet mall, when you're leaving a voice-mail message or explaining your position, when you're flirting with a fella or salting the soup, stop just before you want to, just before what you think the stopping point is. That way you'll never overstep it.

4. Find ways to deal with your stress that won't distress you later. Do deep breathing or read something that makes you laugh. Talk a walk or a power nap. Call a friend or dial-a-prayer. Do anything except revert to a self-sabotaging default.

5. Never walk out the door without remembering who you are. If you think poorly of yourself, there's little reason for *not* getting back with the guy who treated you badly or eating the better part of a pie. Be sure, then, that you're holding yourself in high esteem before you go out into the world with all its choices and temptations. When you consciously remember that you came to this earth to further the plans of the universe, you'll treat yourself as someone who matters that much.

6. Frame every response in your favor. The idea is to get to the point at which saying no to something that is not for your ultimate benefit feels as good in the present as it will in hindsight. Once, in my teens, chatting at an airport with a girl about my age, I offered her one of the cookies I was scarfing down. She said, "No thanks, I'm way too

15

hungry to eat sweets." At that moment, I both detested her and wanted her to move into my head and be my conscience. She was hungry, but she cared enough about herself to wait for a real meal, and she framed her response to the proffered goody in a way that made her seem mature, together, and decidedly cool.

The attentive chaperone who goes through life with you from childhood to old age will help you respond to assorted eventualities with the same finesse that young woman had. You can reframe "I would so love to have this, but I could never afford it" as "This is lovely, but I'd rather get more for my money." Or replace "I'd give anything to go with you, but I'd better put in some overtime at my hideous job" with "Thanks for asking, but I'm working my way up to CEO."

Not even the best inner chaperone can prevent all regrets, nor would she want to, but your knowing she's in there will help you prevent many of them. Like your inner epicure, she is an ally who's always on your side.

Lucky Charm

The next time you question whether something
you want to do or are asked to do is right for you,
let your inner chaperone weigh in on the matter.

5

Wake up and smell the morning

*In the morning, you're presented with
all manner of possibilities.*

One of my favorite books, *Invitation to a Great Experiment,* by
Thomas Powers, bears a most unusual frontispiece: a life-sized
photograph of an alarm clock. This seems like an odd image with
which to introduce a book about coming to know God (the "great
experiment" of the title), but the author contends that if you want
to do something of this magnitude, you have to get up an hour earlier than usual and spend this hour, in his view, with equal parts
physical exercise, prayer and meditation, and reading something
enlightening and uplifting.

If you try this, I think you'll see that it is a great help, whether
you are out to experience God or simply feel divine. The early-
morning time gives you a head start and a decided edge. If your
office opens at nine, your co-worker who sleeps in till eight has
time for only a quick shower and a gulped coffee before showing
up (probably frazzled) at work. If you get up at six, you can meditate, work out, do a nice job on your hair and makeup, and eat

a real breakfast before clocking in. Who do you think is going to have a more relaxed and productive day?

You may be thinking, "No way I could get up that early." You might even believe that you are a night person. I am here to tell you that you *learned* to be a night person. You are not a cat or a cockroach, an owl or an opossum. As a human being, you can see only in the daylight (or in the artificial daylight we've had for less than 150 years). When you learn to get up early, 7 a.m. at the latest, you give yourself the full expanse of morning, the freshest time of day.

The ranks of successful people are filled with early risers. Contemporary examples come from business (e.g., Donald Trump), sports (Andre Agassi and Monica Seles), and spirituality (Deepak Chopra). Historic early birds include Benjamin Franklin (he coined the ditty "Early to bed and early to rise makes a man healthy, wealthy, and wise"); the nineteenth-century poet Walt Whitman and his precursors from antiquity, Horace and Virgil; and even the fellow who gave us the ability to stretch day into night, Thomas Edison.

You can join this august group. Set your clock fifteen minutes earlier than you're used to. If you're young (under forty, give or take), allow yourself two weeks to acclimate to this slightly altered schedule. If you're older, it can take the body longer to adjust, so give yourself a month. Then inch the alarm back another quarter hour. Keep this up until you're arising at the time that gives you the greatest opportunity for living all day every day.

When you awaken, don't jump right out of bed. Lie there a minute or two. Be aware of the wisdom your soul wants to reveal to you in that delicate place between sleep and waking, when you're least resistant to this kind of guidance. My awakening subconscious has proffered solid business advice ("Call so-and-so today . . .") and help with my health. During my last stubborn cold, I awakened one morning with a strong message: "You need to sweat!" I had a steam bath that afternoon, and my symptoms were gone by evening. Coincidence? I don't think so.

You owe yourself the gifts of the first morning hours. Watch the sun come up. Walk barefoot in dewy grass. Inhale deep gulps of the air that, even in a big city, smells clean and pure at this time of day. In the morning, you're presented with all manner of possibilities. Don't miss a minute of it.

Lucky Charm

19

Tonight set your alarm for fifteen minutes
earlier than usual. Slowly edge it back until
getting up early is just what you do.

Expect the best

The Law of Expectation is,
simply put: those who look for miracles
get them; those who look
for something less get that.

When I was fourteen years old, I believed that I was supposed to meet the Beatles. I didn't just want it: I expected it. Even though I was fourteen instead of twenty-four, and lived in Kansas City instead of London or on one of the favored coasts, I expected this meeting to happen and never doubted that it would. When I learned that the Beatles were coming to town, I contacted the editor of a teen magazine in New York about writing a story. She in turn contacted the Beatles' press agent, and by the end of the week an invitation to the Fab Four's press conference arrived via registered mail.

On the big day itself, however, I ran into a snag. A dozen off-duty police officers were stationed in the hotel lobby with a single mission: to keep teenagers—*all* teenagers—out of the conference room. To them, my official invitation was no better than a forged document.

But I was supposed to be there and I knew it. As I contemplated this obvious (to me) fact, I spotted Charles O. Finley, the promoter who had bankrolled the Beatles' concert, approaching the elevator with a Playboy bunny on his arm. He was headed for the press conference where I was meant to be. I ran up to him and his curvy companion and breathlessly announced, "Mr. Finley, I have an invitation and a press card. I'm supposed to be there."

He looked me up and down, from the cowlicks to the acne to the extra thirty pounds I'd attempted to conceal with a well-intended interpretation of "mod" fashion that had just missed the mark. "OK," he said. "You can come with us. Just don't say anything." I took his un-bunnied arm and became a little part of history—a quiet, plump, and pimpled part, but a part nonetheless. It didn't even surprise me. I *expected* to be there.

I spent the rest of my teens meeting most of the rock groups of the era and writing stories about them. When I was seventeen, Paul McCartney called me by name and bought me a drink. I knew then that I had a charmed life. It would be years before I understood that what I'd tapped into as a less-than-cool adolescent was a principle that could bypass cool and go all the way to awesome. I'd happened onto the Law of Expectation. It is, simply put: those who look for miracles get them; those who look for something less get that.

Since then, in my studies of the mystical part of life, I've learned that there are laws about how things work on a spiritual level just as there are laws such as gravity, mass action, and thermodynamics that govern the physical world. Most people know about some of these spiritual principles. Take, for example, the Law of

Karma—cause and effect—or the Law of Attraction: the vibratory current you put out into the world via your thoughts and feelings draws to you experiences of a similar vibratory frequency. (We'll touch on these again in chapter 46, "KC, Here I Come.") The Law of Expectation is one more such principle, and it's the one most active in the experience of people who live what we call charmed lives. They expect to land on their feet, and, despite disappointments and detours that may crop up along the way, they somehow always do.

Here's what you need to know. The Law of Expectation, like any spiritual law, doesn't negate plain old physical laws, nor does it turn earth into heaven and humans into angels. What it does is present you with what you genuinely expect—not just wishin' and hopin' and thinkin' and prayin', but what you expect at the deepest part of yourself. When you expect fulfillment and a life that becomes more meaningful as you go along, that's what you'll get.

You can start to consciously use this law by figuring that little things will turn out OK. You might expect, for example, that you'll catch your train right on time. But on some particular morning, what do you know? You just missed it. So you expect to meet someone fascinating who also missed the train. Or use the extra waiting time to read an article you wouldn't have otherwise. Or call a friend who needed to talk to you more than you could have known.

In other words, expect the best, not some totally unrealistic version of it that you can't really believe, but the real-world *best* that could, without your winning any lotteries or running into a wish-granting genie, happen for you. Once you start to see this law acting in your life, you can work up to even more impressive aspirations, because those will now be believable, too.

23

Some people shy away from this idea because they think that if they expect great things and end up with something mediocre or worse, they'll be disappointed. This is faulty logic. Have great expectations. Anything else that happens between here and there is simply part of the process. Calmly respond to exigencies. Put out fires as necessary. And keep expecting the believable and the wonderful.

Lucky Charm

Look at your schedule for the day ahead. For each task and appointment, hold the mental image of everything working out beautifully.

24

7

Give something away today

The process of going around
and coming around
is sweet and sure.

My friend Sherry and I drove five hours each way to attend a seminar on enlarging our prosperity consciousness. The presenter was Paula Langguth Ryan, who has devised a twenty-one-day program in which participants are to become so positive it would disgust mere mortals. One of Paula's action steps asks attendees to give something away every day during the three-week period. I found the practice to be so freeing that I've kept it up. In fact, I hope that when I die it will be in the afternoon or evening, so that even on my final day on earth I'll have had the chance to give something away.

Back in the '60s, some hippie philosopher advised people to "go with the flow," but nobody ever said what this *flow* was. I figured it out through the exercise of giving something away every single day: the flow is giving, giving and receiving. When I give without expecting a return (or even a thank you), I keep the channels open for the flow of good to come to me and through me back out into the world.

If you find this intriguing, try it today. What you give is entirely up to you. Maybe it's something of yours that someone else really likes. Years ago, my friend Alima had an eye-catching wall hanging that said, "When you're being run out of town on a rail, get in front of the crowd and make it look like a parade." After I'd commented on it the second or third time, she turned around, took it from its hook on the wall, and said, "It's yours." I was thrilled, and I enjoyed its cheerful colors and gutsy message hanging across from my desk for quite some time.

Then someone I cared about, the minister at my church, whose sermons always spoke to me and whose caring had brought me through quite a bit, came upon hard times himself. Powerful members of the board wanted his resignation because they thought he was doing too much work for peace (no kidding) and they disapproved of his warmly welcoming gay and lesbian members into the congregation. He was, literally, being run out of town on a rail. When it became obvious that he and his wife would indeed be moving to a church in another part of the country, I knew I had to give that wall hanging to this man who had inspired me to live a bigger life.

It gave him a rueful chuckle, and he told me he would take it with him to his new post. I don't know what happened to it after that. He probably gave it to someone else. This process of going around and coming around is sweet and sure. My role in the biography of the wall hanging is not where that little piece of mass-produced art is today, however, but what happened in my soul when Alima gave it to me and again when I passed it on.

Maybe what you have to give right now is something that is still getting you compliments, like those Alima's wall hanging elicited from me. Or maybe it's something that's just taking up space in your house but that someone else could put to good use. You might be moved to give money, even if that means postponing a purchase for yourself. Or perhaps what you have to give is intangible but just as real as a coat you could take from your closet or a bill you could take from your wallet: some minutes of your time, information you have to share, or instruction you can offer. It all counts.

During those initial three weeks of conscious giving, I wrote down the first thing I gave away each day to be sure I wouldn't forget. It started a habit that has resulted in less excess to contend with and more access to both the solid and ethereal accoutrements of a charmed life.

27

Lucky Charm

Give something away today, or daily
for three weeks, or every twenty-four hours
for the rest of your life.

Behold the thousand-pound gorilla

The sizable primate
that blocks charmed lives
is usually a single issue that is
so enormous we prefer to pretend
that it doesn't exist at all.

A lot of people work very hard to get charmed lives for themselves. They'll implement suggestions from this book as they did from *Creating a Charmed Life* and the many other helpful books and blogs, audios and DVDs designed to bring about the *aha!* that changes everything. When their efforts don't seem to pay off, however, some become discouraged and start to believe that while charmed living may be an option for the fortunate few, they're not in that group.

This is particularly regrettable because the answer is often so obvious. What stands in the way is a thousand-pound gorilla: that presence in the room (or, in this case, in a life) that you can't miss— *unless you want to.* The sizable primate that blocks charmed lives is usually a single issue that is so enormous we prefer to pretend that it doesn't exist at all. Consider these examples:

- ❦ You detest your job and always have, but you've invested time in it and you don't want to lose the benefits.
- ❦ You know you drink every day and sometimes too much, but the word *alcoholic* sticks in your throat.
- ❦ Something horrific happened to you a long, long time ago, but you've never been able to talk about it, even with your husband or a therapist or your closest friend.
- ❦ There's something you've longed to do for decades, and that desire won't leave you alone, but going for it would upset a whole fleet of applecarts.
- ❦ You're in a relationship with someone who doesn't treat you well, but he's sexy and has a great job and your mom and dad like him.
- ❦ You're living a lie, pretending to believe something you don't or feel enthusiastic about something you no longer do.

Any one of these, or any one of a thousand predicaments like them, can derail all your other efforts. If there is a thousand-pound gorilla anywhere in your life today, take a serious look at the big guy, the real problem. It doesn't matter what circumstance or set of them seems insurmountable today. Once you acknowledge that the big beast exists and that it's in your way, you're on the road to overcoming it.

If you're dealing with a thousand-pound gorilla, here's a little field guide:

- ❦ *Do away with any shame you're feeling.* Nobody gets through life without running into a thousand-pounder, and many of us have come upon two or three or a whole colony.

❀ *Get your head out of the sand.* If it feels like a problem, it's a problem. Face it, and get whatever help you need to deal with it.

❀ *Don't rationalize.* We can tell ourselves that nobody's life is perfect and that this situation isn't really that bad, but if it comes to mind while you're reading this chapter, it probably is that bad.

❀ *Don't compensate.* Making more money or keeping your house cleaner or coming down a dress size won't negate the fact that there is thousand-pound gorilla keeping you from claiming the charmed life that has your name on it.

❀ *Find the help that's out there.* Go to friends, go to professionals. There is somebody who can help you; you don't have to do this alone.

❀ *Use the strength you gained facing one major issue to tackle the next one.* Having a thousand-pound gorilla leave your life for other habitat does not mean that another one won't emerge. It doesn't seem fair that you should have to confront yet another great ape when some people seem to sail through life with only the occasional spider monkey. Nevertheless, the energy you spend thinking about fairness is energy that could go toward dealing with the situation at hand as you so admirably dealt with the previous one.

❀ *Remember how much you're worth.* Reread chapter 1, "Know That You Are Worthy." Having to work your way through a difficult challenge does not diminish your worth in any way. If anything, it enhances it by making you stronger

31

and wiser and better able to help someone else in a similar predicament.

For every person who is living a charmed life because she came to earth with a free pass to all the rides, there are thousands delighting in charmed days and decades because they made peace with one or more thousand-pound gorillas. You may not know that this was in their history, but if you ask, chances are they'll tell you all about it.

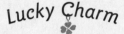

Lucky Charm

If you've been evading the biggest issue
in your life, find a way to face it.
Once you straighten out the situation with
King Kong, the rest will be relatively easy.

9

Admire all your aspects

How can we expect ourselves
to find the best in people
of other cultures, religions,
and ways of life
if we can't accept our own
diverse characteristics?

My husband has a friend who is a business executive, a Jehovah's Witness, and a serious Harley rider. I love that! I also know a financial planner who is about to have a TV show and who also runs a restaurant; and a teacher who tends bar for extra money so that every few years she can go to India and be a full-time yogini. It's so easy to rail against these descriptions: "Motorcycle guys do not read the *Watchtower!*"; "Yogis have no business making margaritas!" This is because putting people into a mold is easier than allowing for their individuality. Allow for it anyway, because then you'll allow it in yourself.

It's not always easy to accept and admire our own divergent aspects, and other people can be downright miffed about them. Even those who swear that they're not the least bit prejudicial have preconceived notions etched in granite: Artists are starving. Successful people are cutthroat. Activists are extremists. Idealists are unrealistic. Attractive people are shallow. The list goes on and on. The problem arises when one of these folks runs into an attractive, successful, artistic, idealistic activist—you, for instance. They don't know where to cubbyhole you, so they just let you know what aspects of yourself they find unacceptable. You can't control those people, but you can accept yourself—every part of yourself.

We know the importance of embracing diversity at work and in our communities. People are different, and together we make up the intricate patchwork of humanity. How can we expect ourselves to find the best in people of other cultures, religions, and ways of life, however, if we can't accept our own diverse characteristics? Which parts of you don't conform to the other parts? What is there about you that surprises people and sometimes surprises even you? Admire your uncanny ability to house so many marvels, and refrain from passing judgment on some off-the-wall trait that is an improbable but utterly endearing dimension of your uniqueness. Swami Kripalu wrote, "Each time you judge yourself, you break your own heart." Admire yourself instead, you and all your parts.

Spiritual teachings from around the world tell us that learning to love is the primary reason we come to earth. This lesson is hardest when it comes to loving ourselves, but there's no passing the course without it. The enticing amalgam of characteristics that comprise your personality and your character—every crotchet and oddity and imperfection included—is a lovable and laudable thing.

Being multifaceted does not mean that you're "all over the place." It means that you are capable of bringing together seemingly mismatched elements in the form of a fascinating human being. You are complex and richly textured, and if somebody finds you difficult to label, good. You weren't looking to be labeled anyway.

Lucky Charm

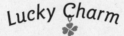

What is the wackiest part of yourself, that aspect that seems to be a gene from the milkman? Admire it today. Enjoy it. Put it to good use.

Make life-charming decisions

If anyone who has ever lived
was capable of creating a charmed life,
you're capable.

If you're serious about this charmed-life business, you must make certain decisions. These are watershed resolutions, as difficult to go back on as the decision to join a convent or the army. I'll list them here like a quiz in a magazine: which ones can you check off right now, and which ones have you yet to make?

I've decided to:

See life as a magnificent adventure. If you see it as anything less than this, it will be less than this, and that's too bad.

Know that I can do this. If anyone who has ever lived was capable of creating a charmed life, you're capable.

Go it alone if I have to. This doesn't mean divorcing your husband or disowning your parents (although I suppose in extreme cases it might). It's about taking the charmed-life path on your own if no one in your immediate circle believes that this is possible (for you or for them).

Make my mark. We won't all be known in the eyes of the world, but we'll all know what we did with our lives. When you decide to make your mark, you embark on the road to fulfilling your unique destiny.

Take risks. Go ahead and go for it. Somebody will catch you. A song I really love, "Grateful," by John Bucchino, has a line that says: "There's a hand holding my hand. It's not a hand you can see." Know this for yourself.

Be disciplined. Lazy people don't live charmed lives. Know what you need to do today and do it. No excuses.

Become a seeker. You're practical, ambitious, and have both feet firmly on the ground. Excellent. But without looking into the philosophical and mystical underpinnings of all that is, you miss out on the grand and the glorious.

Live in the biggest possible world. Travel. Get to know people from many different places. Read the literature and history of other cultures. The bigger your world, the richer your life.

Care profoundly. To help the environment, we want a smaller carbon footprint, and to help others, a bigger *caring* footprint. In practical life, this means seeing things through others' eyes, sharing resources, and shopping with conscience—asking, Where does this come from? Who made it? What is its history?

Listen to my instincts. That's why you have them. They're dependable. Practice inner listening. Until you know what's what, run your intuitive promptings past a trustworthy confidante who'll help you tell the difference between wishful thinking and the wisest counsel you'll ever receive.

Appreciate everything. It's one thing to be grateful for the good stuff, and that's a fine place to start. For an exceptional life, however, you'll want to be grateful for everything: the hard lessons, the gray days, the detours that looked as if they were going nowhere but ended up taking you precisely where you needed to be.

Be in this for the long haul. You're aiming for a charmed *life*, not just the occasional good day. You're going to adopt certain attitudes and practices and use them for as long as they benefit you, even if that's forever.

Lucky Charm

Make one decision today that solidifies your intention to live a charmed life.

39

11

Bring back chivalry

Chivalry is being the godsent friend or stranger
in a story that goes, "I don't know what I would
have done if she hadn't shown up."

I was impressed that he'd made it down the stairs and onto the sub-way, this diminutive man of some years, obviously in the advanced stages of both arthritis and osteoporosis. On the crowded rush-hour train, he reached for the bar with a misshapen hand and I, also standing, was aghast that no one occupying a seat offered it to him. Just before the car lurched forward, another man, looking to be over seventy himself, arose so his elder could sit.

Now, I grew up on fairy tales and movie musicals. They taught me to expect a world populated with heroes and fairy godmothers, with men dedicated to righting unrightable wrongs and women ca-pable of climbing every mountain. That evening on the train, the only valiant figure had white hair and bifocals, evidence of the fact that chivalry is an endangered quality.

Because it is one tall order to live a charmed life in an uncharm-ing culture, it's up to each of us to bring back chivalry, updated for our times. Today's "knight in shining armor" can be male or female, and the "damsel in distress" could be a child or an animal, a man or a woman. In day-to-day affairs, this means allowing yourself to see a need when one exists and, if you're capable, stepping up to meet it.

You don't have to fight in duels or scale enchanted towers. How about stopping to help someone whose grocery bag breaks, or the embarrassed fellow shopper who's just knocked over a towering display of bathroom tissue? Or talking to the bored little boy in the post-office line while his mother chats on her cell phone? Or giving a hand to the stranded motorist trying to change a flat? (If you can't change a tire, here's an assignment: learn this simple skill within the next seven days. You cannot be chivalrous in this day and age without knowing what to do with a lug nut.)

Reduced to its fundamentals, chivalry is being the godsent friend or stranger in a story that goes, "I don't know what I would have done if she hadn't shown up." It's a way to change the world for the better, one kind act at a time. This contributes to exalted living, because it heightens the meaning of your days and the impact of your time on earth. And it charms the lives of other people, many of whom may see very little magic and wonder in their quotidian affairs.

To bring this full circle, learn also to accept the chivalrous offerings of others. On that train, I thought back to the few times in the past when someone had offered me a seat and I'd responded with a self-sufficient, "Oh, no, I'm fine." I was fine, but no one enjoys having a kindness rebuffed. Perhaps if I—and everyone else who had ever said, "Oh, no, I'm fine" in this situation—had instead smiled, said thank you, and accepted the seat, one of those erstwhile knights would have more readily come to the elderly gentleman's aid.

Finally, take the time to encourage acts of chivalry in your children and grandchildren. It may be a lost art, but there's no reason we can't find it, reinstate it, and make it the norm. We may not help anybody to "happily ever after," but "happily all afternoon" is something I think we can do.

Lucky Charm

*Be on the lookout for opportunities to save the day,
even in so small a way as being the one to provide
a tissue or a pen. Do this routinely until chivalry
becomes second nature.*

43

Wash the dishes
with all your heart

In a charmed life, the best thing going
is what is happening now.

Even the most dazzling lives are punctuated more by commas and periods than by exclamation marks. You virtually guarantee a charmed life when you can give yourself as fully to doing the dishes, and tending to the other miscellanea that make up your day, as to some grand adventure. This is because you can count on the dishes. They'll be there alongside the grand adventures, and if no adventure is immediately forthcoming, the dishes won't let you down. Besides, feelings of enthusiasm, excitement, and positivity about anything and everything attract adventures to a life the way an open bag of trail mix attracts bears to a campsite. They just can't stay away.

About fifteen years ago, I picked up a severe case of flu while traveling, and it kept me in bed for a month. I'll never forget the first night I washed dishes after I was better. It was the most satisfying experience: warm water halfway up to my elbows, and slippery, shimmery suds to play in. I momentarily wondered if the high fever had addled my brain—I mean, please: dishes?—but if it took being addled to feel this content, I didn't want it any other way.

During the first few weeks of getting back into life, I was having these sublime moments during activities once inconsequential in their ordinariness. "Wow, driving a stick is really fun! . . . What did they put in this hot cider? It's *amazing*! . . . The sunset was so beautiful I pulled my car over to look at it." Smitten with my new way of seeing things but questioning its normality, I called one of my mentors, a woman named Gladys Lawler, who was nearing ninety and always knew the answer.

She told me that these simple occurrences seemed so stunning because I was in the moment. "When you're in the moment," she explained, "everything is exquisite because you're truly experiencing it." Life, I learned from Gladys that day, ought to be this way all the time, but we're so used to being removed from the present by keeping our minds in one place and our bodies in another that these periods of resplendence are uncommon. She also told me that I'd be back to the old, disconnected way of being before long, but that since I now knew that being truly present was possible, I could remind myself to go there again.

Her prediction was correct. As soon as my full strength returned, I was back to busy mode: scheduling, planning ahead, multitasking. But even now, the otherworldly beauty of that convalescent time can come back when I'm washing dishes. I have a dishwasher these days, but I often use the sink just the same. It gives me the opportunity to stand in one spot and focus on one cup, one glass, or one perfectly circular rubber gasket that, in its modesty, gives me the use of my blender.

I recommend that you try some conscious dishwashing. Release all judgment ("I always get stuck with the dishes . . ."), and just be with the process. Run the water and be aware of the sound it makes rushing from tap to sink. Look at the bottle of soap before you squeeze: What's in it? Do you like how it smells? Watch the suds as they build and billow. Pick up a dish at random—your coffee mug maybe, or the bowl your daughter used for cereal this morning—and regard it as a gift from a grab bag. Perhaps it has something to tell you, something to remind you of. Be with it and with every subsequent plate and fork and measuring cup until the task is through.

Then give yourself just as wholeheartedly to whatever comes next. In a charmed life, the best thing going is what is happening now, even when it's scouring a skillet.

47

Lucky Charm

The next time you do the dishes,
feel the water, caress the crockery,
and be present with all that's in you.

Dress for the occasion

Clothes come and go,
but wearing them appropriately
will get you a reputation for knowing
how to do things right.

People used to dress for the occasion, whatever it happened to be. I
for one believe that was a good thing. What you were wearing helped
you know where you were and what was expected. Things are different now. For a great many women, jeans and sweats are basic
attire and "dressing up" means putting on the pants that have to be
dry-cleaned. Obviously, we're not going to return to an era when
every event had a dress code, but if you assign flexible standards
of attire to the recurrent events of your own life, you'll feel more at
ease and more confident. You'll be silently giving a degree of respect
to those around you and contributing to the ambience of wherever
you are, whether that's the opera or the Little League game.

Clothes come and go, but wearing them appropriately will get
you a reputation for knowing how to do things right. People will
assume you know a lot about a lot of things merely because you

show up at the various venues of your life attired for each situation. And you will retain an air of mystery and intrigue. Because dressing appropriately has become a rare thing, people will wonder who you are!

While you're at it, make a note of some wardrobe tricks that can make you look as if Audrey Hepburn or Princess Diana bequeathed you her style manual. Start with these suggestions for:

Dressing for a Charmed Life

Oh, chapeau! Every woman can carry off some kind of hat, and most of us can look smart in two or three styles. Once you're able to wear a hat naturally and you're not thinking, "There's something sitting on my head," you've passed Millinery 101. Find every store in your area that sells great-looking hats and check them out. Look at vintage shops as well: hats from the days when a lady never ventured out without one can be the very best.

Black tights/black flats. Think *French woman.* When you let opaque black tights create an unbroken line with your shoes, your legs look longer and slimmer, and you've given comfy flats the elegance of heels.

Real accessories. Maybe it's your great-aunt's delicate watch or an estate-sale stickpin. If that's not your style, how about Native American jewelry, Georg Jensen silver brooches, or a beaded amber necklace? Real jewelry needn't be out of anyone's price range if you expand your definition of *real* to include natural materials that are not as precious as gold and gemstones.

Less is more. In business, 20 percent of the effort is said to produce 80 percent of the profit. In your closet, chances are that 20 percent of your clothes are worn 80 percent of the time. Get rid of the fillers! They're just taking up space and wrinkling the good stuff. Don't be afraid that you'll downsize your wardrobe until you have the proverbial "nothing to wear." That lament comes when a woman looks in her closet and can't see the things she loves because of all the not-so-great pieces that are hiding them.

The right bra. I was once at an all-female business dinner when a woman in our party, a bra expert, casually mentioned that I could use "more separation and less out front." Out front! I was appalled. But also intrigued. Would the right bra change everything? No, but it would (and did) change for the better how I looked in everything I owned. Find a shop with a bra lady who's been trained to use a tape measure and interpret its findings. Buy the bra you're told is right for you, and discover the difference.

Tailored to perfection. Few of us could get jobs as fit models, women who are a "perfect" size six or ten and on whom the sizes are tried out. If the sleeves need to be shortened, or the shoulders taken in, or the waist let out a bit, allow someone skilled with a needle and thread to work some sartorial wonders. Tailoring is not expensive, and it can make "off the rack" (even off the sale rack) look custom-made.

Serendipitous shopping. Recreational shopping is passé, but shopping to make a necessary purchase should be a pleasure. In a charmed life, you're neither overwhelmed at the thought of buying clothes, nor prone to shopaholic binges. Keeping your wardrobe adequate and attractive is simply one delightful task among the many you enjoy. With this attitude, you *expect* to find the piece you're looking for. (It's that Law of Expectation again, this time in a very down-to-earth guise.) You trust that you'll know "it" when you see it, and when there's a time crunch, you trust that *now* (or within ten minutes) is when *it* will appear.

I used this technique the day of an important business meeting. The blouse and jacket I was wearing didn't seem right. I had just half an hour to spare, and the only place to look for a new top was a store that was so expensive I'd never thought of it as a practical place to shop.

Undaunted, I found the floor housing the bridge lines (designers' offerings with prices low enough not to need a comma), determined that something was there for me. When I got off the elevator, I saw that major sales were taking place. I picked up a couple of potential items and then I saw the one that I knew was mine: an understated pullover in soft gray, with slender stripes and delicate beading in steel gray and black. Bingo! It fit perfectly and was offered at a mere quarter of its original price.

I wore it out of the fitting room, and as I was settling up with the salesclerk, she commented: "That sweater is so right for you, it even matches your ring." I looked at my right hand and saw a ring my mother had left me, a black onyx stone in a carved silver setting. I'd never had it on until that morning. Sometimes serendipity precedes us, even in matters as minor as buying a sweater.

A treasure here and there. The investment doesn't have to be huge. Thanks to seasonal sales, outlet stores, sample sales, and consignment shops, designer apparel is far less "exclusive" than it once was. Besides, you don't need a wardrobe of it, just a piece here and there. Black pants, for instance, as long as they fit well, are just black pants; there's no need to look (or pay) for designer detailing or quality. The special jacket you wear with them, though, could be with you for years and is therefore worth every dollar you spend on it.

When you are wearing something spectacular, however, be sure to remember that you are supposed to outshine your clothes. I have a light blue jacket that I bought to wear on TV. That special, professional reason for having it gave me the courage to spend more than I ever had before (or since) on something that I couldn't either drive or move into. A glimpse of that label, even after owning the jacket for eight years, can still make me gasp. For a long time, I treated this garment like a modern-day Joseph's coat, taking it to a luxury dry cleaner because I'd convinced myself that no one else could iron the collar right. It was only when I got over all that and was willing to pop on the jacket with a T-shirt and jeans—in other words, treat it like a piece of clothing instead of a holy relic—that it was really mine.

Selecting appropriate clothing and getting a kick out of wearing it is a joy you so deserve. It's not a matter of size or price, but rather of putting something on and feeling special in it. When you lose any discomfort you may have around choosing clothes and what to wear when, you'll feel better about your body and about yourself. And you'll know with all that's in you that life is too short to ever wear sweats unless you plan to perspire.

Lucky Charm

Go through your closet this weekend. Take everything that doesn't make you feel beautiful to Goodwill or the Salvation Army.

14

Slow down

When we take our time,
we have more of it.

You can sip life slowly like fine wine, or gulp it like cheap beer. As a reformed gulper, I recommend sipping. Life has a pace of its own, one we're prone to abandon for other timelines and other clocks: the alarm clock, the time clock, the biological clock.

These urge us to hurry along. If we're parents, we hurry our children, which is a pity, because in a twinkling they'll be hurrying themselves. We skimp on sleep, eat on the run, and think about the next obligation while we're still engaged in this one. We juggle commitments as if we're planning to audition for Cirque de Soleil. In rushing through our checklist and careening through the check-out line ("Yes! Today I picked one that's moving for a change"), we miss the enchanting fine points of our own lives.

The antidote to "more to do than time to do it" sounds para-doxical: *instead of speeding up, slow down*. I learned this many years ago from a fellow eighth-grader named Joy. While all the other girls were stressed to the max to get dressed after gym class and make it to next period on time, Joy acted as if she could spend all day in the locker room. She took her time dressing, carefully dried and rebraided her hair, and even organized her books and papers so she'd be on top of things for Spanish and math.

It made no sense. She had the same seven minutes as everybody else. Some of us tried to analyze how she did it. Joy belonged to a very conservative church so she didn't wear makeup, but we determined that the braiding time made up for that. Perplexed, one day I just asked her. "The Lord held the sun for Joshua," she told me. "I figure He'll hold the bell for me."

I was dumbfounded. I mean, everybody thought of Joy as off-the-charts religious: she carried a Bible, wore below-the-knee skirts, and planned to enroll in an unaccredited college that didn't teach evolution. Her belief system and lifestyle differed from mine quite a bit, but on this matter of time something was working for her that wasn't working for me. So I began to act on her conviction that if I slowed down, time might stretch for me like it did for Joy and Joshua. And for the rest of the year (and in ninth and tenth grades, too, until I could get through the dreadful PE requirement), I was always on time to my next class, with dry hair, both shoes tied, and my shirt tucked in.

Even today, when I remember Joy, I think to pace myself. To slow down. Take it easy. Do less but be present while I'm doing it. This is one of those spiritual verities that operate on a kind of logic that is more metaphysical than physical. There are several of these: when we're generous, we have more money; when we're humble, we get more admiration; when we give up the struggle, we find the solution; when we take our time, we have more of it.

Once you get used to it, slowing your pace feels so good that it becomes easier to eliminate demands on your time that don't have a good reason to be there. I know we all think we have a million things to do. But ask yourself: "Out of the million things, which three or seven or ten will really make a difference for me, for my family, or in my work? And out of the three or seven or ten, which really require attention today? How much ease could I add to this day if I focused my full attention on one task, one pleasure, or one person at a time?"

Once you decide where you will put your attention, give that attention fully. And if you're interrupted—the phone rings, the baby wakes up, everyone who's ever wanted anything from you suddenly wants it now—give each request that same attentiveness. Breathe into the moment, and place yourself firmly, fully, in the now.

57

As slowing down moves from experiment to habit, you and time will become congenial colleagues—no more fighting it, no more fearing it. You'll know you have this down when you find that you're reading the whole Sunday paper—the magazine, too—and you're so caught up on your work that you can take off a Wednesday afternoon for a Gilbert and Sullivan matinee. This is how life works when you slow down, sip it, and inhale the bouquet.

Lucky Charm

Cut today's to-do list in half, and trust
that it won't cause the world to end.

Stay close to what makes you come alive

You do the most for someone else
by staying connected
to what keeps you glowing.

If I weren't committed to keeping the chapter titles in this book succinct and positive, I would call this one: "Never, Ever, Under Any Circumstances, No Matter How Good a Reason You Think You Have, Give Up What Makes You Come Truly Alive or You Will So Regret It." I'm not telling you this because I read it somewhere and it made sense. I'm telling you this because I've done the opposite and I know that when you give up something that makes you come alive, you can still breathe and walk and apparently function, but you cut yourself off from inspiration and joy—the exact materials you need for building a charmed life.

After my teenage stepson, James, died, and William, my husband, was in such pain and grief, I wanted to help him any way I could. In retrospect, I see that just standing by him was all the help I had to give. In my own grief and confusion, however, I decided that if we left New York City and moved to a small town upstate, the change of scenery and the simpler life would somehow make this difficult time a little easier for him.

I already knew that leaving my home of seven years would be rough. New York City isn't just a municipality to me: it's a state of mind. Opening my shades in the morning and seeing the Chrysler Building always gave me a surge of energy and delight. Even when certain things weren't going as I wanted, I could hang on to the fact that I had made it to the Mecca of writers and dreamers for the past two centuries. Now I was going to leave it behind for what seemed to be a higher purpose.

Things did not go smoothly. (When this happens, by the way, pay attention. Something that you're very much meant to do may involve a few obstacles, but if you find yourself on a veritable obstacle course, life is trying to tell you that you're off track.) Anyway, I plowed ahead despite ample indications that I was nuts. By the time we'd given notice on our Manhattan apartment, rented one in Woodstock (local vendors sell T-shirts that say "Woodstock: Midlife Crisis Capital of the Northeast"), and leased a car, there was no turning back. We went forward with our relocation to another planet, a mere hundred miles away.

Woodstock is a charming artists' community in the Catskill Mountains, and the eponymous concert (which actually happened in the town of Bethel, some fifty miles away) has kept the 1960s alive there in glorious, living tie-dye. It should have been just right for me, but like the guy who left his heart in San Francisco, I'd left my life in New York City. It took me a couple of months to understand that in my genuine desire to be supportive of someone I love like crazy, I'd become oblivious to the obvious: *If I lose my spark, who am I helping?* We both soon realized that small-town life would be only a year's hiatus for us, and we'd figure out what to do with the other twenty-four months on the car lease when the time came.

Ultimately, things worked out. We moved from Woodstock to the providential Harlem condo I told you about in chapter 2, showing me once again that even our less prudent exploits have a way of righting themselves, morphing into teaching tools and bestowing us with experience, the very currency of a lifetime.

Even so, you can learn and grow either with suffering or without it. Contrary to the beliefs with which many of us grew up, "without" is preferable. That's why you want to be careful every time you think you're being noble and magnanimous by giving up something that makes your heart sing like the Vienna Boys' Choir.

61

Now, let's understand each other about what makes hearts sing and people come alive. What lifts you up to high-level liveliness is an individual call. No one besides you can tell you what is or is not in this category. We are, however, talking about real, soul-molding stuff, not casual preferences. You may, for instance, truly adore walnut brownies, but letting Aunt Minerva have the last one on the plate doesn't count as giving up something that makes you come alive. Putting another's needs first at times, whether in matters of dessert or something more momentous, is a necessary part of life and maturity. When you sacrifice your connection to joy, however, it's like donating your second kidney. This is the point at which generosity turns into self-destruction.

Something that works a great deal better is to identify those people, places, and things that sustain you like air and water and three squares a day. Your list will comprise the human beings (and maybe dog/cat/other beings) that make up your inner circle; a place or two or three on this globe where you either need to reside or touch base periodically; and those few pastimes and even fewer objects that you would have a hard time living without. Once you know what these are, refuse to give them up. They sustain you and you need them.

Sometimes circumstances intrude and shorten the list: A person who's on it dies or moves to Brazil or falls in love with somebody else. You get transferred to another city, or your knees age before the rest of you and the long-distance running that kept you so jazzed has to go from habit to history. You may even have some valid reason to give up something dear for someone dearer, but be sure when you do this that your loss will truly be your loved one's gain. Sacrifice for its own sake is not just overrated; it's a con. In the vast majority of cases, you do the most for someone else by staying connected to what keeps you glowing. That way you can shine your light into the other person's dark places. Otherwise, nobody will be able to see, and you'll both bump into the furniture.

Lucky Charm

List the people, places, and things
that make you come vibrantly alive.
Stay as close to these as life will let you.

Become surprisingly fit

"You can't buy muscle.
The only way to get it
is to build it yourself."

We all know that to be healthy we need to maintain at least a moderate level of fitness. Because the majority of Americans aren't doing even that, I realize that I'm offering a challenging proposal in suggesting that you set your sights on becoming not just reasonably fit, but surprisingly so.

Why this overachievement? Because you want an extraordinary life. Having an extraordinary body will help you get that life and be up for its rigors once you're there.

Don't fall for the cultural norms that define this kind of body, though. I'm not talking about the *Sports Illustrated* swimsuit issue. What I'm putting forward is that you become as strong and conditioned and flexible as is possible for you, given your heredity, age, and lifestyle up to now, as well as any physical limitations you have to work around. Sure, doing this will mean that you'll look trimmer and tighter and you'll have muscle definition that people will envy, but those are just garnishes, like parsley on a plate.

The point is, when you know that you have strength and endurance and flexibility beyond what's expected, you may appear to be a mild-mannered hairdresser or physician or second-grade teacher, but there's a superhero underneath. You might not leap tall buildings in a single bound, but you can run for the bus, climb over a fence, move the couch, and let your cronies on the cruise go to napkin-folding class while you climb the rock wall.

Even your brain will function better when your body is in this kind of condition. *And you did it on your own.* You can hire a personal trainer or purchase state-of-the-art workout equipment, but as sought-after New York City trainer Sasha Lodi told me: "No matter who you are or how much money you have, you can't buy muscle. The only way to get it is to build it yourself."

A lot of exercise programs entice would-be consumers with "You don't even have to go to a gym!" But if you want a surprising level of fitness, you do have to go to a gym. Of course it's *possible* some other way, and it's possible to become a millionaire by begging on street corners. It's just not efficient or likely. Even athletes who swim or ski or run nearly every day also make it to the gym several times a week to be as toned and trained overall as they are for their particular sport.

Gyms are everywhere and some (like the Y) are quite inexpensive. Join one. Then defy the odds and actually go. (According to the Web site healthandfitness.com, only one in five health-club members shows up twice a week or more.) Here is a three-part plan for getting to this elite level of fitness with a relatively small time investment:

1. Do cardiovascular exercise (the treadmill, stair-climber, ski machine, dance class) five or six days a week, half an hour each time (that's twenty minutes plus a five-minute warm-up and a five-minute cool-down).
2. Engage in resistance exercise (weight training) by alternating twenty-minute upper- and lower-body workouts five or six days a week. (Working your abs fits in here, and you can tend to those muscles every day.)
3. Perform a series of gentle stretching moves after every aerobic-and-weight-training session. Ten minutes is enough.

This program gets you in and out of the gym in an hour, plus the time it takes to shower and dress, which you'd have done anyway. If you're up for more, add one or two yoga classes each week for additional suppleness and grace, and improve your core strength, back health, and six-pack potential by supplementing your daily abdominal crunches and curls with a Pilates class.

Get your doctor's clearance for all this exercise if you're over forty, if you've been sedentary, or if you have any health conditions or old injuries that might call for an abridged or altered program. Enlist your mate or a good friend as a workout partner so somebody is counting on you. Eat high-quality food and enough of it: no puny-girl diet can fuel the kind of body you're crafting. "Enough" means that you're satisfied from meal to meal, and you're not dropping more than a pound or two a week (or losing any weight if you don't have it to part with).

Get plenty of sleep at night; this is when your cells take all the work you've done and make something out of it. And take one day a week off, sometimes two. On these days, get a little extra rest. Luxuriate in an Epsom salts bath. Let your body recuperate and incorporate what you've done all week.

Is this more than most people will do? It is. And you may well have only moderate fitness as your goal right now, which is fine. Just remember that you aren't reading *Living an Average Life*. I encourage you to go for the gold—body and spirit.

Lucky Charm

Get to the gym today.

17

Seek out your life stories

Our stories aren't about what happened
nearly as much as how we feel
about what happened.

Poet Muriel Rukeyser said, "The world is made up of stories, not atoms." I think the poet in all of us would agree. Indeed, an often overlooked but essential charmed-life skill is choosing your stories. Find them by noticing the magic in the moments and the details of your life. Look for the humor in whatever is going on and places to laugh at yourself. If you can't extricate yourself from a situation that would make a bad story, reframe it as a cautionary tale. And when you're in the midst of a really good story, pay attention. It's a masterpiece.

For instance, I was driving in the country and came very close to learning how well my side air bags worked when a careless motorist came out of nowhere at warp speed. I was about to engage in road rage—except that just before I blew my top, I saw a woodchuck on the side of the road. I'd pulled over to recover from the collision that hadn't happened and was in the perfect spot for watching this adorable creature munch on the greens that he held in his darling little hands. I'd never been this close to a woodchuck, and I had a decision to make. I could do road rage (I was about to call my husband and regale him with the unabridged account of my narrowly escaped death), or I could do woodchuck. Woodchuck won. It's a better memory and a better story.

As you come to regard your life as a series of narratives, you sometimes get a really great one. When I was on my last book tour, I'd left home without a manicure. Since nail salons are on every block in New York City, I figured that would also be the case in Portland, Oregon, my first tour stop. I wandered around Portland's very alive and attractive downtown but didn't find a nail salon until I got to the outer edges of the central business district—nothing fancy, but it would do.

Entering, I saw a single employee, a young man working intently on a model airplane. (So that's what they do with the glue left over from the sculptured nails! Who knew?) When I asked about getting a manicure, I could tell that he thought I was interfering with the progress of aviation, but he agreed and we got started. The silence was uncomfortable, so I tried to initiate a conversation. My questions garnered disinterested, monosyllabic answers until I asked the right one: "What is this music you're playing?" He lit up. "This is salsa," he told me. "You have come to a dancing city."

He went on to explain that when he wasn't working, he was dancing: salsa, ballroom, and tango. "When you learn to dance," he explained, "you can finally hear the music. You hear how the rhythms go up and down and you know that life has rhythms, too, and you learn how to go with them. And when you dance with a partner, you learn to move with their rhythms and their motions, and then you start to know how to get along with anybody. And, ma'am,"—he got really serious—"we would have peace on earth today if all the world leaders knew how to dance." I waited a minute to make sure he wasn't kidding. He wasn't.

By then I was filed and buffed and polished, and he came around to escort me to the nail dryers. I don't like those contraptions (I think the UV light causes age spots), but I had nothing to worry about, because we never made it to the nail dryers. Instead, we stopped in an open area at the center of the salon. I didn't know it yet, but this was the *dance floor*. He put forth both his hands and said, "First, we learn rumba." I'm thinking, "This is so cool." So we did it: slow-quick-quick, slow-quick-quick. It was fun. I didn't trip or kick him or do anything embarrassing.

69

When the song ended, he stood back and scratched his chin. "You're pretty good," he concluded. "I would usually never do tango on the first lesson, but since you're only here for one day I'll make an exception." He changed the CD and came back, positioning me in the classic stance: one arm straight out, man's hand on woman's waist. That was heady in itself. Then the music began. At the first note, he became Antonio Banderas, and I was Madonna, and it was *Evita*—and although I would ask Argentina not to cry for me, I knew it would.

I must tell you that I've never been much of a dancer, and I'm certain, in retrospect, that in that brief introduction to the dance of love, my moves were laughable. But that's not how it felt. And our stories aren't about what happened nearly as much as how we *feel* about what happened.

Well, songs don't last long, and I had a reading to prepare for, so I paid for my manicure and collected my gear. My short-term dance teacher suggested that maybe when I went back to New York I could go to Chinatown and get him some bootleg salsa CDs. I told him I'd see what I could do, knowing that I'm too upstanding to buy counterfeit CDs but that to say so would have spoiled the moment. So, I returned to my regular life with nice nails that would last four days and a story that would last forever.

Charmed lives, like the poet's world, are made up of stories. You'll live them as you look for them and take in their nuances. Seek out—and be open to—the stories of your life: the funny, the poignant, the instructional, the inspiring, and those that carry a reminder that there is more to life than what we see. Then share your stories with the people who really want to hear them.

70

Lucky Charm

Bring to mind your "signature stories," those that, when woven together, make up the fabric of your life. Give each one a simple name (e.g., "Woodchuck Story" or "Dancing in Portland"), and jot down the name in your serendipity log so you'll remember each one. Then go out looking to live another entrancing story.

Live richly

Anytime there's a wolf at the door
(or growling on your voice mail), it's hard to
focus on bringing your dreams into being.

You do not have to *be* rich to live a charmed life, but you do have to *feel* rich, confident that you have enough for what you want to do today and that more is coming for what you'll want to do later. This isn't such a difficult concept when you realize that money is pure, useful energy waiting for a clear-thinking human to use it in ways that will bring more ease to the world. If you have enough, that's good. If you plan to have enough, that's good, too.

Mystic and theologian Charles Fillmore once said: "Poverty is a sin." I clearly remember my horror upon hearing this as a teenager. I thought he had some nerve to imply that poor people sinned more than rich people, and my youthful sense of justice was outraged. I mean, didn't everybody know that rich people were more likely to be greedy, selfish, and generally more adept at sinning than the hardworking poor, who patiently endure their fate and make sure the earth stays salted? But I was sixteen and had yet to experience either life or lack. After exposure to both, I've come to understand Mr. Fillmore's point: poverty itself is the sin because it keeps those in its grip from being all they can be.

And we're not talking just abject destitution either. Anytime there's a wolf at the door (or growling on your voice mail), it's hard to focus on bringing your dreams into being. If you're in debt or you have no financial reserves, you aren't free to donate to your favorite causes or take a month off and volunteer somewhere. You may not see this as a sin, but it is certainly a shame. Therefore, it seems that we could use:

A Charmed-Life Approach to Finances

72

Live beautifully on what you have now. People whose souls thrive on simplicity can live elegant lives on relatively little cash. They exploit the low- and no-cost riches tucked away in the library, resale shops, and beauty schools. They find treasures on eBay, and ways to barter for just about anything. They know the showtimes for movies with bargain matinees, and they can tell you when it's free day at all the museums and galleries.

One caveat: even doyennes of the unpretentious need sufficient wherewithal to support their chosen lifestyle. Spending Saturday afternoon at the library is delightful, but not if you're there because they've turned off your heat. (By the way, some of the people who live in this frugal fashion are wealthy. They simply like simplicity—and they like holding on to their money.)

Stay in the black. Debt is diabolical. I know that almost everybody has it, but there was a time when almost everybody had bubonic plague, too. A fixed-rate secured loan for a house or a car is one thing, but if you're in credit-card trouble, give up those cards the way an alcoholic in recovery parts ways with the booze. For help with that, or if you see no way of paying off your outstanding debt, check out Debtors Anonymous. You'll meet people there who once owed more than most of us will ever see, paid it back, and now live in abundance.

Even if you're not a chargeaholic, it's smart to get down to one card and pay it off every month; you'll have your debit card for backup and crisp currency for daily expenses. You know the travel slogan "What Happens in Vegas Stays in Vegas"? Adapt it for your finances as "What Happens in the Month Stays in the Month."

See yourself as a natural-born earner. Barbara Stanny wrote a book called *Prince Charming Isn't Coming: How Women Get Smart About Money.* I recommend the book, but if you only remember the title you'll be the better for it. Maybe you're not expecting a literal prince (or a guy with a trust fund) to change your financial state, but if you find yourself contemplating lotteries and long shots, replace the unreal fantasy with a very real vision. *You can make money.* See yourself doing it, and keep your focus on making more as you go along.

In any work you do, give greater value than what you're paid for. Learn to ask for raises, or, if you're self-employed,

73

keep your rates competitive but don't discount yourself out of business. Look for ways to expand your professional life.

Steer your career with foresight and good sense. This ever-changing world is not the one in which our parents and grandparents came of age. Then, any good worker could expect forty years, a gold watch, and a decent pension. We've lost that security, but what we have instead is the opportunity to use a variety of our talents and explore a variety of our interests, to develop new skills, and to follow through on our entrepreneurial inclinations.

Pay yourself first. It's a trite expression, but it holds up: pay yourself first. Take a percentage off the top and divide it into three savings categories: (1) prudent reserve (at least six months' living expenses to carry you through a job loss or unpredicted large expense), (2) retirement, and (3) special purchases. Having that prudent reserve is probably more important now than ever before in our lifetimes. There aren't a lot of guarantees out there: build your financial cushion and be your own guarantor.

Employ the "wealth secret of the sages." If you've read my other books, you know that I'm a proponent of tithing, giving 10 percent of your income to the charities and religious/spiritual organizations that make your soul soar when you know you're part of their work. Men and women who do this prosper. And when it comes to feeling rich, nothing gets you there faster than knowing that you're able to share.

Create your own economy. My grandmother used to tell me, "Millionaires were made during the Great Depression."

They figured out how to create a micro-economy that worked when the larger economy didn't. Do the same in any economy by providing a product or service people will pay for in good times and bad.

Demystify wealth. Read the business section. Take continuing-ed classes on personal finance, investing, and real estate. Know enough that when you're given professional advice, you'll be able to weigh that advice and accept only what sits right with you.

Also, let your emotions learn the ways of wealth by sitting in the lobbies of fine hotels and doing some "just looking" in grand department stores. Regardless of how much you have to spend or where you plan to spend it, nowhere on earth is "too good" for you. When you can move effortlessly between Tiffany and Target, and exercise prudence in both places, the world is yours.

75

Lucky Charm

Find among your friends someone who also wants
a charmed financial life. Get together with your
respective laptops, bank statements, credit-card
bills, and calculators. Figure out how much you're
worth, how much you owe, and what you're going
to do to improve the ratio. Support each other
to see the process through.

Prioritize the people who matter

These are the individuals
who are there when things are toughest
and who will be there when everyone else
has something more pressing to do.

The people who matter may not be the ones you think—the movers and shakers, A-listers, and people who know people and could put in a word for you. The people who genuinely matter in any life are those who make up its innermost circle: family members (particularly those who make you feel so good about yourself you'd have chosen them if you could have), and the close, close friends who compose what some would call a *soul group*. These are the individuals who are there when things are toughest and who will be there when everyone else has something more pressing to do. They're the people for whom we, too, are supposed to show up, in large and small ways, till death do us part.

As important as these friends and relatives are, it's sometimes more difficult to share important feelings and experiences with them than with acquaintances or even strangers. The challenge to overcoming this paradox is to get to know our intimates more intimately. It would be a simpler task if we humans weren't so adept at erecting invisible walls to protect ourselves, the way medieval cities had ramparts to keep out invaders. Although our walls serve a purpose—you don't want to be on a familiar basis with everyone on earth—they also impede our developing more closeness with those relatively few beings who are ours to dearly love.

It isn't possible to deepen the intimacy of a close relationship by mounting a bulldozer and attempting to demolish someone else's barricade. You have to start with your own defenses—lowering their height, perhaps, or adding more doors and windows that allow access to your heart and soul and history. How? By sharing something of your deepest self with a person you can trust to know you fully and love you anyway.

You also get to know the celebrities of your own life better by taking some one-on-one time with each of them and doing something you both enjoy. Whether it's your life partner, your child or your parent, a sibling or a really good friend, when the two of you get together for a dinner or a weekend, you forge bonds that can't be built in a group setting.

After Adair got married—she was young by today's standards (twenty-two) and had been living at home—I wondered how those mother-daughter times I cherished so much would change. What I've found is that they're less frequent now and we have to plan them, as in "What does your calendar look like for a week from tomorrow?" As it turns out, this booking ahead seems to make our get-togethers all the more special. Usually we meet for coffee (her) and tea (me), or we go to lunch or to the park with the dogs. A

78

couple of times a year when I'm speaking at a spa, she comes along. Discussing the relative merits of the Shiatsu treatment and the hot-stone massage helps us get to know each other in our respective life phases and can lead to deeper conversation.

Whatever it takes for you to stay close to those who mean the most, do it. Get to know these Very Important Persons as they are today, and let them know you. Take the time. Make the effort. The people closest to you are the best gifts life hands out. By all means converse with the stranger in the doctor's waiting room, and share your views with the acclaimed and powerful should you get the chance. Invest your hours and your energy, however, in those first-tier folks, the ones for whom you, too, are a gift like no other.

Lucky Charm

Make a date with one Very Important Person
in your life. Repeat regularly with this person
and/or another VIP.

20

. . . Then connect with the rest of us

*People make things happen
for other people,
and the vast majority of us feel good
when we help someone else.*

A recluse, if he likes being a recluse, can no doubt have a quietly charmed life all his own. But it's easier for those who are connected to other people. If we are indeed all one in a spiritual sense, it stands to reason that life would work best when we are making contact with others in those wonderful "I know you and you know her and she went to school with my brother" kinds of ways. In business, making these connections is called *networking*. In a charmed life, we can think of it as *interweaving*—looking for connections, expecting to find them, and letting yourself feel as pleased as punch about each one.

I look at every person I meet as someone who's been put in my path by divine appointment. I never sit next to the "wrong" person on a plane or train. Unless one of us is working or reading or sporting obvious earphones, we talk. This person has had experiences I haven't and knows things I don't. We may not stay in touch or ever meet again, but for that span of time, I grow a little from being in the presence of this teacher.

When you don't have ready access to as many helpful and fascinating folk as you'd like, reach out. One of my friends heard a successful businessman say that if you make ten calls a day, your business will improve to such a degree that you won't even recognize it in three years' time. Inspired by the prospect, she and I started doing what he said, reaching out to ten people a day. I promised myself that at least half of the ten contacts would be by phone, leaving the rest for e-mail and Internet liaisons when those seemed more appropriate. I called all sorts of people: those who were successful in my field and in totally different fields, people I knew but hadn't spoken to in a while, and others I'd met only once but whose cards were still in my file.

My life changed from day one. I don't think I was prepared for people to actually get back to me. When it started happening (and it started immediately), I was suddenly caught up in a whirlwind of positive energy, with one person introducing me to another, inviting me to this and that, and generally catalyzing possibility into actuality. I also found in contacting these people that some of them needed a piece of information from me or some assistance I could provide. It was without doubt a double win.

People make things happen for other people, and the vast majority of us feel good when we help someone else. Still, it can be intimidating to reach out to someone we don't know well (or at all). We could get caught in a maze of voice mail and gatekeepers, and the person, even if we do get through, could deny our request or blow us off as though we don't matter. There's a word when that happens: *Next!* There are plenty of people out there, and if one isn't willing or able to help, there are nearly 7 billion others waiting in the wings. If you want to try this, just take a deep breath and pick up the phone.

It isn't all about asking either. The other side of making contact is what it can do for the other person. In addition to the calls you plan to make and the e-mails you plan to send today to enrich your life or improve your business, how about some reaching out to a person or a few people who would simply love to hear from you? Surprise somebody: someone you haven't talked with in a long while, someone who's lonely or down, or someone who simply loves you to pieces. They're waiting for your call.

83

Lucky Charm

Contact somebody who may be able
to help you with the biggest dream you've got,
and contact somebody else
who'll just be thrilled you called.

21

... And sometimes savor solitude

It is in solitude that we're most likely
to get our novel ideas
and brilliant hunches.

As pleasant as it is to be with people you adore and meet those you find interesting, it is in your solitary moments that you compose your life. Although you may have an outgoing personality and love to socialize, you won't have a complete sense of what you're about until you can also savor solitude. This is because you have within you the ability to live remarkably and accomplish great things. Without some time alone in which to discover it, however, this germinal power is apt to stay right where it is. Instead of tapping into it to enrich your time on earth and make a difference for the rest of us, you'll take it to your grave.

Unfortunately, our era and culture misunderstand the role that periods of seclusion are meant to play. We put children in "time out" for misbehavior when "time out" ought to be a reward—some precious minutes to be with one's own ponderings, unencumbered by obligations and expectations. It is in this time apart that we come to ourselves to regroup and to reconfigure who we are. As we interact with people throughout the day, we take on others' opinions and ways of seeing things. In solitude, we get to process these imported viewpoints and determine whether we wish to keep them, edit them, or eighty-six the lot. And while social settings invite witty repartee, it is in solitude that we're most likely to come up with our novel ideas and brilliant hunches.

Think about your own life and where within it you find patches of privacy and peace. These might be first thing in the morning before anyone else is up (refer back to chapter 5 for tips on early rising); when you go for your run; the train ride to and from work (there are other commuters, but you can still be alone with your thoughts); or lunch hours—especially those you take in the park or in a quiet corner of your favorite cafe. If you use them well, these times to yourself that already have a place in your day can be enough.

You'll probably use a portion of your alone time to read or listen to music, but sometimes it's good to simply be with yourself, to let your thoughts wander and see where they go. If you use some of this time for interior pursuits such as prayer and meditation, you turn passive solitude into active solitude, consciously investing it in your personal well-being.

Charmed-life ladies and gentlemen also find ways to get extended solitary stretches once or twice a year. There may be some times in your life when this isn't practical—if you're single with small children, for instance—but most of the years you live will allow for a weekend in the mountains or a week at a retreat house. Singer-songwriter Alice Marie Bergman filled me in on a solo weekend she gave herself at a suburban hotel: "I watched *Sex and the City* reruns, bought Carrie Bradshaw—looking shoes, and caught up on much-needed sleep and daydreaming. I also took stock of all that I've done the past six months and got clarity on what's coming up."

If you can't see yourself taking off alone to the Holiday Inn, know that some of the most rarefied retreats happen at home when your husband or roommate is away and you get to spend Friday night, Saturday, and the full sweep of Sunday in your own good company. While going away gives you the gift of a new environment, staying home lets you be in your own cherished space. You know where everything is. Just forget where the mop and the washing machine are: you're on re-*treat*.

In this, as in all good things, moderation is the rule. Solitude is delicious, but isolation is dangerous. If you find yourself overly fond of the safe confines of your own home and your own self, get out into the world and appreciate its bedazzlements. The whole point of having cloistered times is to put to use what you learn from them. You do that out in the stream of things, out where people can be grumpy and traffic can be stalled and you can be a bright spot in somebody's day.

87

Lucky Charm

Get away by yourself sometime today
and savor those moments.

22

Add a splash of red

Red is the charmed-life color because it lets
the world know that you're here
and that you deserve some attention.

You can look sunny in yellow and pretty in pink, but red takes guts—not just for attire, for life. If you're going out for a smashing good time, you don't say, "We're going to paint the town purple." When you get half a dozen strokes of luck in a twenty-four-hour period, you don't say, "That was a blue-letter day." For such occasions, only red will do.

Indigenous peoples around the world and throughout history have believed in the ability of red to protect them from harm. In the West, the color is a sign of love and passion, and in the American flag it represents courage and valor. The Chinese say that red invites luck, wealth, and fame. A feng shui practitioner will tell you that giving your home appropriate dashes of this most visible hue will invite more happiness, enthusiasm, and celebration. She may also give you a red envelope in which to put her payment: cash or a check so presented is believed to multiply the largess and call in more good fortune.

Red symbolizes energy. I read years ago that researchers had found that exercisers who wore red leotards (how long has it been since you saw *that* word?) had more stamina. It's also known that the mere recognition of this vibrant color quickens the heartbeat and boosts metabolism. Psychologists say that people who are especially fond of red are go-getters who can accomplish more before breakfast than their peers do all morning, and whose timing on everything is "full speed ahead." Even those who prefer to stop and smell the roses would do well to stick their noses in a few red blooms.

For all these reasons, I think of red as the charmed-life color. Wearing it and living with it tells the world that you're here and that you deserve some attention. This doesn't mean "red all over" like the old newspaper riddle. A few well-placed splashes can fill the bill. You might try:

- ❀ *Red shoes.* It's not just girls from Kansas who get to wear ruby slippers.
- ❀ *A red wall.* Painting an entire room red would soon grate on the nerves. One wall *en rouge,* however, can increase the energy in your home and magically raise the bar on your aspirations. Consider the wall just opposite the entry to the house or to the room; this is the feng shui position for "fame and reputation." Watch out for red in the bedroom, however: a little bit (a rug, a candle, a picture frame) is good for romance, but an entire wall could interfere with sleep.
- ❀ *Red lips.* I'd long worn a conservative brownish lipstick or the pale pink gloss often recommended for women who've

reached, well, a "certain age." But when I went to the cele-
brated makeup artist, Mercedes, at New York's John Barrett
Salon for my every-four-years "head shot makeover," she
suggested a no-holds-barred red. It was instant glamour,
and what an ego boost! I felt like a movie star, "certain age"
or not. Try it—and be prepared to stop traffic.

- *Red nails.* There's a widespread belief, I think, that good
  girls wear pale polish. With red, you can give the good girl a
  break and be a fascinating, mysterious, and daring woman.
  (Red nails and lips at the same time is too much of a red
  thing—unless perhaps you're wearing all black and very
  little jewelry. And you have confidence to burn.)

- *Red flowers.* Having one bud in a delicate vase, a stunning
  dozen roses, or a few red blossoms in a mixed bouquet
  picks up the energy wherever you place it. (And if you're
  really feeling your oats, sport a jaunty red carnation in your
  lapel. I dare ya.)

- *A red gem.* Whether the real thing or a costume piece, a
  ruby ring, bloodstone brooch, or garnet necklace can provide just enough crimson to make you memorable. These
  stones were traditionally used to protect against the evil
  eye. They can at least protect us from a lackluster day.

- *Red accents.* A teakettle or napkins. A lampshade or a throw
  pillow. The ribbon in your hair or the leash on your dog.
  Red is potent. It doesn't take much.

If you're having any uncomfortable feelings around all this red
talk, try to identify what's at the root of those. Red does not have

to be your favorite color, but if you're reluctant to put a little of it here and there, this could signify an unwillingness to be seen. Start small, with tiny touches. You have a lot to offer this extremely needy world, and only when it can see you will it know what you have to give.

Lucky Charm

Splash some red into your life today:
something to wear, something at home,
something at the office.

Grow green gracefully

Be sure there's something in this
for you. Otherwise it's too easy to revert
to the way things used to be.

I remember when and where I learned the word *ecology*. A year out of high school and living in London, I was exploring a marvelous, musty bookshop called Watkins when I came upon an entire section of books that looked at the earth as a living organism.

In retrospect, I see that during the eminently charmed year I spent across the Atlantic, I lived in a more ecologically sound manner than ever before or since. I didn't drive. I had no refrigerator and bought food daily from small markets and street stands. There wasn't an air-conditioner in my student digs, and I used the heat only a few hours a day because I had to put coins in a meter to run it. On cold nights when I ran out of change, I learned the warmth-conserving value of thick curtains and thick socks.

At the time, living like this seemed normal. Now I realize that it *was* normal in a way that the plastic-bagged, drive-three-blocks-for-paper-towels way of life I came from had never been. That still hasn't made it easy to return to the simpler, more sustainable way of life I'd taken to so easily as a young expatriate. In the years since, my attempting to live in accordance with an environmental ethic has sometimes felt like deprivation, or simply like a whole lot of work that I shouldn't have had to do when almost nobody else was. Other times it seemed like a fad: "Green is the new black." Today I see that living with respect for the planet is less an option than a moral imperative. It's helped me to look at going green the way people sometimes look at growing older: gracefully, and with a sense of excitement about discovering new alternatives to familiar products and practices.

You can find "Top 10" and "Top 50" lists of tips for going green all over the Internet. I recommend your checking these out and adopting as many of the suggestions as you can over a reasonable period of time. I'm in the process, too, ever modifying the way I do things. The daily changes are minuscule, but a decade's worth are substantial, and as more and more of us make them, we form a groundswell.

Reordering everything overnight can be too radical and, as a result, short-lived. Because so much is riding on these changes, they need to be strong and solid—bricks in the foundation of your lifestyle. And—here's the clincher—you have to feel good about each new habit you implement. As Sophie Uliano writes in the introduction to her book *Gloriously Green,* "If I make one tiny positive change today, I consider myself green. It can be as simple as flicking off a light switch or buying an organic apple." This is smart psychology, because if you consider yourself green, you'll make choices to support that assumption. If you don't resonate with one

of these changes, if it seems like a hassle or an imposition or a hard-
ship, skip it for now and do something else instead. You want these
lifestyle revisions to last. You want your children to see them as fun
and fine and ordinary, as "just the way we do things."

Start by thinking about the environmentally savvy steps you
already take. It could be that recycling is second nature to you, and
you installed a water-conserving showerhead so long ago you don't
even remember that it's there. Perhaps you always fill a water bottle
from your five-gallon jug or the purifier on the tap, and you shop
with cloth bags because it seems silly to toss out either paper *or* plastic. Maybe you've cut way back on your meat consumption since
learning that animal agriculture releases even more greenhouse
gases than automobiles.

Whatever you do or plan to do, find a way to get a kick out
of it. Grow a garden if you love gardening, and be a regular at the
farmers' market if you don't. Have fun shopping for kitchen towels,
cloth napkins, and fountain pens you'll fill with ink and keep forever instead of the plastic toss-aways. If you enjoy finding these at
secondhand stores, you get extra credit, but if you're not there yet,
no problem: you're doing a lot.

Should you start taking the bus to work, rediscover the pleasure of reading en route. As you acquire fewer possessions that
don't mean much, you'll see how nice it is to buy something you
really want. And as you get savvier about shopping with the earth
in mind, you'll come to see that there are so many green choices
nowadays that you can select the one that serves your needs and
suits your budget. Settling for an inferior product because it's the
conscientious choice is no longer a step that has to be taken. And

although organic and recycled products can still cost more than the conventional option, the price gap is narrowing as greater numbers of us look for ways to take the best possible care of our bodies and our planet.

All in all, see these changes as adventurous and creative. Otherwise it's too easy to revert to the way things used to be. But things are the way they are now. We can either hide from that, resent it, or devise for ourselves and our families the classiest eco-savvy life going.

Lucky Charm

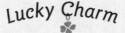

Make one change a week to bring the way
you live more into harmony
with what the earth can accommodate.

96

24

Keep your sunny side up

Look for light in the darkness.
If others aren't seeing any
and you've found some,
you're like the one person in a blackout
who has a working flashlight.

"Look on the bright side." "Think positively." "Just change your attitude about that." Those chipper people can be really annoying when you know that everything is going to hell in a picnic basket and anybody who didn't have his head in the clouds would see that, too. And yet, when the memorable moments and charmed lives are being allocated, it's those positive-thinking bright-side-lookers with the changed attitudes who are routinely called to the front of the line.

This is because we see what we look for. Positive people who respond to "How are you?" with sentiments like "I feel great! Business is booming! Life is wonderful!" are not unaware of the challenges in their own lives or the suffering in the world. They simply choose to focus on the flip side: "Challenges can be overcome.

Suffering can be alleviated. I'll take what actions I can today to be part of the solution."

Circumstances come as they come and they're not all pleasant, but when you're able to revamp your reaction to circumstances, you alter the trajectory of your life. The way I see it at this point is that I have two choices: I can either be negative, sophisticated, and miserable, *or* I can keep my sunny side up, seem to some people a bit of a lightweight, and be happy. Today I'd rather be happy. If you would, too, up the positive factor and see how it opens the door (and windows and gates and skylights and crawl spaces) to greater happiness.

Listen to your words and thoughts. When you hear yourself making some downer statement, whether audibly or inside your head, stop immediately and package it some other way. You might, for example, open your shades in the morning and see clouds and rain for the fifth day in a row. Your knee-jerk response could be "Another crummy, depressing day!" Change that pronto. Turn it into "What a great day for reading that novel! . . . Terrific: I don't have to mow the lawn . . . A little more weather like this and I'll have the complexion of a twenty-year-old." This is not denying reality; it is, rather, looking for and acknowledging the positive elements that lie within even what seems negative.

Admittedly, we can face situations far more dire than a series of rainy days. Even in these cases, though, it's possible to look for light in the darkness. In fact, you owe it to everyone involved: if they're not seeing any light and you've found some, you're like the one person in a blackout who has a working flashlight.

This kind of attitude adjustment attracts good things the way a Yard Sale sign attracts bargain hunters. It is not, however, a combination magic wand and miracle drug. Sometimes having a great attitude is all it takes to draw what you want into your life. Other times it allows you to live with grace and contentment when you haven't gotten what you want.

There's more to this than whistling in the dark. It's a disciplined way of thinking that primes the brain to come up with answers to nagging questions, ways out of troubling dilemmas, and the means for processing circumstances differently. With that renewed mind-set, you can see a situation that would have seemed dreadful as merely demanding—demanding of the best you've got: your smarts, your courage, and the sunniest outlook you can summon.

Lucky Charm

99

Have a keynote thought, one positive idea to set
the tone for your day, first thing every morning.
You might try "It's wonderful to be alive" or
"I already feel the good this day holds for me."
This thought is independent of circumstances.
It isn't wonderful to be alive because you just got
the raise or the last 38-C on the sale table, but
because you've been given a day that is,
by definition, filled with possibility.

Take such good care of yourself

Nurturing one tiny part
of the Divine in expression—
yourself or myself, for instance—
increases the bliss in the universe.

I recently had lunch with my friend Consuelo—a quick lunch because I had a lot to do. There is probably a Consuelo in your life, a woman with enormous, liquid eyes—eyes that tell you what she's going to say before she says it. On this day, after I explained how hard I was working, her eyes looked especially loving when she said, "Remember, when you take care of yourself, you take care of the universe."

I got the message, and also an intriguing concept to ponder. You see, unlike those with a CliffsNotes take on such esoteric fields as quantum physics and string theory, Consuelo has studied these as a scientist. While I may *believe* that I'm a speck of the Divine, she has made a life's work of coming to understand how this could indeed be the case. And she helped me understand that, just as making an improvement to the smallest room in a house increases the value of the property as a whole, nurturing one tiny part of the Divine in expression—yourself or myself, for instance—increases the bliss in (and value of) the universe.

This is not an invitation to selfishness, but it is a clarion call to making your own body, mind, and spirit high priorities. We want to do all we can for those we love, and many of us seem to have a "caregiver gene" that makes us want to look out for everybody. Even so, there are certain needs that must be self-met. No one else can make you value yourself, engage in healthful habits, have fun, pursue your dreams, or seek answers to the big questions about life and God and purpose. It's up to you to take care of your beautiful, complex self in all these ways, or you'll burn out. The meaning will seep out of life in dribs and drabs. Even the good feelings that once came from being so available to other people will diminish as clouds of resentment take their place.

I don't deny that real-world exigencies can make it difficult to care for yourself to the degree that you deserve. Raising children demands that a portion of the nurturing you'd have once given yourself now needs to go to them, and you wouldn't have it any other way. Still, if you're a single mom or you have a special-needs child or other extenuating circumstances, what's left to nurture yourself can get to a critically low level. Having the responsibility for aged parents, especially if dementia is involved, can so exhaust your caring capacity that when you do get a break you don't want to care for anyone, yourself included. Even job stress, especially if it's intense and unrelenting, can diminish the normal desire to self-nurture, and mental states including grief and depression can come close to shutting it off altogether.

When one of these conditions or something similar is a part of your life, self-care can seem peripheral and trivial. In fact, not only is it necessary in its own right, but it can help you get through what you're going through. Taking one small step in this direction, doing some brief kindness for yourself, can have far more power than the act itself would seem to generate.

Let's say you decide to take a walk. That self-nurturing thought leads to another: bring your iPod. So you walk for half an hour, listening to an inspirational talk you uploaded months ago. You come back refreshed, physically and mentally—for the time being at least. And that refreshment brings with it what refreshment always does: creative ideas—for a practical way to ease the tension at work maybe, or a simple system for ordering the papers that seem to be multiplying on your desk and seeking world domination.

Taking good care of yourself leads to taking better care of yourself. This happens automatically because your body, mind, and soul are interconnected, and when you do a good turn for any part of yourself, all parts benefit. You don't have to start with some kind of high-maintenance, diva-style personal upkeep: just be nice to yourself. You'd do as much for a loved one, a friend, and probably a stranger.

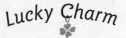

Lucky Charm

Do something today that makes you say,
"I'm taking such good care of myself!"

Ease the e-mail onslaught

*When technology interferes with moving
your body, contemplating the grand
scheme of things, and relating to other humans
face-to-face, it's time to shift the focus.*

Other than the rare freethinker who's out there to remind the rest of us that individuality is indeed an option, everybody has e-mail. It's convenient, cost-effective, and for most of us nonnegotiable. Because it enables us to correspond with anyone anywhere, it could even be the technology that replaces combat with communication. It is time-consuming, however, especially as e-mail and Web surfing have joined forces as the second great sedentary revolution. (The first was, of course, TV, and we're still watching that, too.)

In addition, e-mail is, by its nature, reactive. People say, "I'm going to check my e-mail" far more often than "I'm going to write some e-mails." You open the mail screen, and ten or forty or a few hundred friends and strangers want something from you. It's wearying to be constantly on call, to know that you've signed on for contemporary "woman's work"—the kind that's never done, except that women, men, and even children are in on this one. As I heard a guy say in a coffee shop, "My memory only goes back two hundred e-mails."

If you love the technology, if it never feels oppressive, and if the degree of it you deal with doesn't un-charm any aspect of your life, you don't need the suggestions that follow. For everyone else:

The Essential Guide to E-mail

Set e-mail hours. You have office hours; have e-mail hours, both at work and at home. You can even include them as part of your e-mail signature: "My hours for e-mail are 9 to 10:30 a.m. and 3 to 4:30 p.m. If your message is urgent, please call." (My rule, which I have admittedly been known to break, is to stay away from e-mail until after lunch and to take Sundays off.)

Become a proactive e-mailer. When you sit down at your computer, *write* the e-mails you have in mind before you *read* anybody else's. Otherwise, you can get so caught up in responding, you forget why you brought your laptop out of sleep mode in the first place.

Do away with constant fake urgency. If your Black-Berry vibrates or your computer beeps every time somebody sends you a one-liner, disable that function.

Answer only what needs to be answered. If you haven't been asked a question and there is nothing you need to say, the note stops here.

In this medium, it's even OK to not say thank you. When someone e-mails you a piece of requested information, your thanks are implied. Writing back to say thanks just gives that nice person one more piece of e-mail to open and delete. It can even start a ridiculous back-and-forth of thank you, you're welcome, think nothing of it, smiley face. . . .

Have two e-mail addresses. Use the first for one-on-one communication, and keep the other for mass mailings, forwarded messages, and to give to any companies that want your e-mail address to send you offers and ads. Saving your primary address for direct correspondence with your actual friends and business associates should keep it fairly clear of spam as well.

Become a ruthless deleter. If there are more than two "Fwd"s in the subject line, delete. If it's in your spam folder and you don't know the person who sent it, even if the subject is something like "It was so nice to meet you," delete. Anyone who really needs to reach you will find a way. Your time is valuable. Delete the e-mail, reap the time.

If certain types of e-mail offend you, politely let the sender know. It's OK to tell people that you don't want a newsletter you never subscribed to or forwarded jokes, poems, pictures, and the like.

When it comes to chain letters, you don't even have to be polite. You've received these, I'm sure: a beautiful prayer or a touching story that at first you think someone actually wanted you to have. In further reading, however, you realize that you and nineteen other people are getting this in order to ensure the sender's prosperity and protect him from some awful fate, which will now befall you if you don't forward this veiled threat to twenty of your other friends. I never pass these on, and I tell the senders why. Yes, I am an inveterate "chain breaker," and no curses have befallen me lately.

Resist forwarding other mailings, too. I know the petition looks as if it could save the world, the virus warning sounds ominous, and the words of wisdom are so, well, wise that you know all your friends should see them. *Refrain.* Take control of your forwarding finger and hold on to this stuff for forty-eight hours. If it still seems worth passing on, go ahead. (Of course, within forty-eight hours you'll have received even more petitions, warnings, and wisdom. It will never stop unless you stop it. Even then it won't stop, but it will slow down.)

Put angry or emotional e-mails into your "waiting to be sent" box. Janice Hunter, a reader in Scotland and a writer herself, reminded me of the wisdom of letting potentially explosive correspondence sit for forty-eight hours. "When you then come to what you've written," she says, "you have more of a sense of how the recipient will feel when he opens it. You may choose to delete it entirely. If not, you've gained some distance and perspective, making it easier to edit an e-mail you do decide to send." (And don't put an actual address on an angry e-mail until after that forty-eight-hour cooling-off period: the message could be delivered inadvertently, hurt someone else, and cause you no end of trouble.)

If you need to write a letter, write a letter. E-mail is great for business communication and short notes. But if you want to catch up with someone you haven't seen in

108

months, or if you're going through a difficult time and you need to pour your heart out to a friend, do it on paper. And when you need to write something really special—a love letter perhaps, or some bittersweet prose for a child leaving home—please make it touchable and savable.

Organize and simplify your Web-based world. Nowadays you're likely to have not only an e-mail account but a blog on which people can comment, and one or more social networking pages where scores of smiling faces are asking to be your "friend." Stay on top of this stuff if it makes you happy, and scale back if it gets to be too much. Above all, keep your real-life priorities straight: your family, your goals, your three-dimensional friends.

Apply these suggestions to texting as well. Since you're forced to keep text messages short, they can be viable stand-ins for e-mail, especially in communicating with the more verbose of your correspondents. If all that beeping becomes just one more annoyance, well, out, damn text!

And through it all, remember the magic. I'm fond of recalling a time when, if I had a writing deadline, I could post a message to that effect on my answering machine, go underground for several weeks, and resurface when the project was finished. I had the freedom of single-minded focus, and no one seemed offended by it in the slightest. Those days are over. With e-mail I, like you, am supposed to be as available as an emergency-room doc. That weighs on me sometimes. And yet, there is a certain wonderment in instant communication and the myriad forms it continues to take. I can hear from someone on the other side of the globe or reconnect with a friend I lost touch with when she moved away after freshman year. Remembering the magic doesn't solve the problems, but it can lift you above them in a rather remarkable way.

Keep in mind that technology, in all its permutations, exists to serve you, not the other way around. It isn't going anywhere, and it's destined to become even more ubiquitous. As long as it enriches your life, it's great. But when e-mail and its kin start to diminish or circumscribe your life with nonstop demands, or interfere with your meeting basic needs such as moving your body, being in nature, and relating to other humans face-to-face, it's time to shift focus. Take control of your time and the quality of your life.

And as you interact with the Internet, keep your powers of discernment keen. We've long been told, "Don't believe everything you read." In the unedited Wild West of the Web, this is better advice than ever. Enjoy the online universe with good sense and a clear head. This is not some 1950s sci-fi flick in which the machines get control of the world. This is your life, the life that just might be asking you to shut off the electronics for awhile and plug back into *it*.

Lucky Charm

*For the next week, chart the number of hours
you spend on e-mail and online.
If the number seems excessive, use the suggestions
in this chapter to get the upper hand.*

27

Put fear in its place

Life is risky, delicate, temporary,
and magnificent. Once you come to grips
with that confounding reality,
you'll be less afraid.

When I feel afraid, I take comfort in bringing to mind the confident voice of Franklin Roosevelt comforting my grandparents and their fellow citizens with the powerful pronouncement: "All we have to fear is fear itself." I wonder if he believed it himself at the time, and if he realized what profundity he'd captured in eight simple words.

Trying to charm a fear-based life is like trying to run a marathon in concrete boots. It can't be done. "I'm scared that I'll never get another job so I just won't look." "I'm afraid there's something really wrong with me so I won't go the doctor." "I'm terrified she's mad at me so I won't talk to her." When dread keeps you stuck, your life is on hold.

I used to think that I couldn't help being afraid. I figured it just happened, like getting sleepy or needing to scratch an itch, but that's only a half-truth. You do get a free pass for that first rush of fear because it's an automatic body reaction. When you see the return address on the envelope or the caller ID on the handset, there is a physical/emotional response based on your past experience with the sender of the letter or the person on the phone. If you perceive a threat, the body responds by releasing fight-or-flight chemicals. Of course, if you're not fighting or fleeing, all that adrenaline and norepinephrine just adds to the discomfort.

After that first response, though, you can put fear in its place by taking appropriate action in the situation, *even if you feel like you're going to die on the spot.* That's the key: knowing that despite what you're feeling, you can deal with this. Those people who keep their cool in a crisis get the same adrenaline shot as the rest of us; they just use it for energy instead of anxiety.

The fear in your life is like the kid at your door selling magazine subscriptions. Both will blow in every now and then, but you don't have to invite them to spend the evening. Besides, a lot of the fear we feel isn't even ours. It's manufactured. There's a part of the human psyche that loves being afraid— thus the popularity of horror movies and death-defying theme-park rides. Because we get a nice tingle from flirting with fear, we talk about it. Chatting about that string of robberies downtown or the threatening weather that may be headed this way makes for conversation that's almost as much fun as gossip. The media doesn't help either. Everybody knows the slogan for local newscasts: "If it bleeds it leads."

And fear spreads like wildfire. We learned in school about the Panic of 1893 and the Panic of 1907, when economic downturns led to runs on banks, causing the very situation people were trying to avoid. The thing they should have feared was—thank you, President Roosevelt—fear itself. And we're not at all immune to this kind of runaway fear in the twenty-first century.

Change is a constant, and change is scary. Dealing with our fellow humans and risking their displeasure is disconcerting. Loving other people and running the risk of losing them is horrifying. But without facing fears like these and changing, dealing, and loving anyway, what's the point? Life is, after all, risky, delicate, temporary, and magnificent. When you come to grips with that confounding reality, you'll be less afraid.

While I am by no means a beacon of fearlessness, I work on it enough that sometimes I surprise myself. I once confronted a man who was sloppy-drunk, wielding a double-barreled shotgun, and threatening to shoot his wife's little dog. (Yes, I called the police first, but they never showed. Happily, puppy and I came out unscathed. The wife, I regret to report, stayed on.)

But it's not the isolated instance of boldness that bestows freedom from fear. It's facing our personal demons. Being criticized maybe. Or speaking in public. Or whatever the newscaster says is today's biggest threat. Your assignment is to face *those* fears and keep on going.

These are the characteristics I've observed in people who don't let fear get them down:

❦ *They whistle in the dark till the lights come on.* In other words, they assume, as I saw whimsically worded on a menu in Reykjavik, Iceland: "Things will be OK in the end, and if they're not OK, this isn't the end."

❀ *They don't exaggerate the situation.* It takes enough doing to deal with what's really going on without gilding the lily.

❀ *They stay in the moment.* The lion's share of fear has to do with something that might happen in the future. Most of the time, in this moment, we really are safe and sound.

❀ *They know how to sit, and they know how to breathe.* While fear sends most people into panic mode, the apparently fearless cut off that response early and instead sit with the fear, inhaling and exhaling slowly and calmly until they get a handle on how to proceed.

❀ *They jump in.* If they have eleven tasks to do today and one is scary, they do that one first. A few times I've separated out my to-dos into a "regular" and an "STD" (scared-to-death) list. If the intimidating assignments are mixed in with the others, I put them off. When they're separated out, I can jump into the scary list like diving into a pool.

❀ *They say no to drugs.* A therapist I used to know called coffee "paranoia punch." Caffeine can cause a susceptible person to be more acutely affected by fear-inducing events or information than if she wasn't "under the influence." Too much sugar has the same effect on some people.

❀ *They remember the genuine pleasure that comes from pushing through fear.* A reader reminded me that in going through that wall, transformation happens. Every time we break through fear to speak our truth or take care of ourselves despite another's displeasure, we generate power we can use to formulate a more charmed life.

114

✤ *They have faith.* Most of the men and women I know who
   have overcome fear have a strong faith in God. The others
   have faith in themselves. They use it to either move beyond
   the fear or take appropriate action despite it.

I pay close attention to these people and emulate them as best I
can. The more often I do what they do, the easier and more natural
it becomes. These teachers have shown me that although I can't
completely fear-proof my life or anyone else's, I can remember that
I've been taken care up until now. I'll get through what scares me
today just as I got through whatever it was that had me shivering
in my boots last time. And every time I bring this to mind, the less
shivering is called for.

115

Lucky Charm
☘

*Whatever is before you today that is
a little bit scary—tend to that first thing.*

Not guilty, Your Honor

*Wallowing in guilt is just a way to dramatize
the past so you never have to let it go.*

You can live a charmed life even if you get discouraged every so often, if your faith sometimes falters, and if your belief in yourself occasionally equals your belief in the tooth fairy. You can do it if you're less than 100 percent positive and if you're not the most disciplined person you know. You cannot, however, live a charmed life if you're burdened by guilt. This is the one mental state that can box you in so tightly that the makings of a charmed life can't get to you. And wallowing in guilt is just a way to dramatize the past so you never have to let it go.

As damaging as guilt is, we still sometimes see it as a kind of absolution. It's common to believe that feeling sufficiently guilty and wretched will make up for whatever we did or failed to do (or whatever we thought we did or failed to do). But it doesn't. In fact, it keeps us stuck so that if there is a past error to amend, we're not able to do it. It's like putting a burglar in jail with no provision in place to repay the victim.

I took a guilt survey. There were no assassins in the group I surveyed, just principled men and women who nevertheless carried around enough guilt that they would gladly have worn hair shirts if Walmart carried them. When I took out their regrets ("I wish I'd traveled when I had the chance") and just left their guilty pleas, I found that what they felt guilty about fell into three categories: (1) youthful indiscretions, (2) selecting one of two imperfect choices, and (3) doing the best they could have at the time.

In the youthful-indiscretion category was guilt about things they did before their brains were fully developed. Children and adolescents can be really mean. For example, my focus group participants told me, "I was really awful to that nerdy kid from down the street" and "I didn't appreciate all my mother did for me" and "I was a bully in high school and can't get the things I did out of my mind."

In category two, selecting one of two imperfect choices, were guilt inducers like "I got divorced and had to watch my kids grow up in a broken home"; "I gave my baby up for adoption"; and "I worked when my kids were little even though I said I never would." But if they'd taken the only other apparent choice, they'd now carry a different guilt: "I stayed in a bad marriage and exposed my kids to that"; "I kept my baby instead of letting people raise her who could have given her what I couldn't"; and "I thought it was great to stay home with the kids, but now I feel guilty that they had a childhood of hand-me-downs and Hamburger Helper."

Finally, in category three, was guilt arising from having a history. Examples I heard included: "I stole my sister's boyfriend because I loved him and I didn't think she did. Of course, we're divorced now"; "I had bypass surgery thinking it was the magic bullet, but I've managed to gain all the weight back"; and "I changed my major in college so I could make more money, but now I feel guilty for throwing away my real gift." In all these cases, and in other instances from your life and mine, we did the best we knew to do at the time or we'd have done something else.

OK, we've all screwed up. Given that, you know what I'd love to see? A giant stadium filled with people, maybe the crowd at a Super Bowl, and during halftime everybody stands up and on a count of three shouts as loudly as they can: "We've all screwed up!" That would be such a healing moment. All those people would come together as one, regardless of which team they were rooting for. And millions of others across the globe would rise to their feet, put a hand on their TV sets, and join in the rousing chorus of having screwed up. We would see the true brotherhood of man because of the solidarity it would generate to come together in this universal admission. We might get world peace before the next commercial.

But do you know what else would happen? Somebody would think about it too much and start to feel guilty. "Oh, my gosh: I *did* screw up. I hate myself. Something terrible should happen to me." And out of that bleak place, he wouldn't want to feel union and practice cooperation anymore. He'd try to make himself feel better by rationalizing that although he was rotten to the core, those other people were even worse. And because our phantom human wouldn't be alone in his inability to keep guilt at bay, we'd be back to where we started by the end of the game.

If you want to know the score on guilt, this is it: it only causes trouble. Sure, we've all screwed up, and if you can accept that as a reason for forgiving yourself and others, you're on the right track.

119

Take responsibility for what you've done or avoided doing. That means that you pay back the money, clean up your act, and do something for somebody else's mother if you want to do it for your own mom but she's not here anymore. Whatever action you take, do it in a spirit of "To err is human. To do what you can about it after the fact is human, too."

When you've done what you can, release the past to the extent you can. Then spring forth into the rest of your life willing to work wonders, make mistakes, patch things up to the degree you're able, and leave the rest to the universal love that's already forgiven each one of us for transgressions that haven't even transpired yet.

Lucky Charm

When you start to feel guilty, make amends, alter your course, and then do something loving for yourself or someone else. It's nearly impossible to express love and feel guilt at the same time.

29

Write yourself a life list

Making the list
helps your assorted dreams
move from pie-in-the-sky
to sweet-likelihood-on-earth.

When my daughter was just seven years old, she handed me a piece of poster board on which she had written "Things I Want to Do" at the top in several shades of Magic Marker. She'd always been precocious, but these entries were especially ambitious and, well, sophisticated—more like a mature adult's "bucket list" and less like a child's "Meet the real Santa" and "See a unicorn" fantasy. Its most salient entries were:

1. Go to Paris.
2. Go to China.
3. Learn to scuba dive.
4. Be in a movie.

I wasn't sure how to respond. I didn't want to dash her dreams, but it seemed that it would take a miracle for any of them to come true. You see, at that time I was a single mom making a modest living writing articles for small magazines. We were living in a tiny rented house in the Missouri Ozarks—quite a distance, both practically and psychically, from any ocean or the Eiffel Tower. Yet Adair was so excited about her creation that I opted for a nonjudgmental, albeit noncommittal, "That's nice." She took that as approbation and hung her list on her side of our single, shared closet.

By the time she was twelve, everything on the list had been checked off as completed. This young girl had learned to dive off the coast of Kauai while I wrote my first "real" (meaning I was paid an advance) book. She'd gone to Paris on the frequent-flier miles earned from having gone to China twice. (My boyfriend at the time had heard about tours to Asia sponsored by a nonprofit group, so we went not only to China but to Nepal and India as well.) Adair had even been in her first movie—a low-budget horror flick that was pretty awful. No matter. Her list hadn't stipulated the quality of the project.

There is something to be said for making a list like this at seven, before our wishes seem foolish or wildly unattainable, and before we know how much things cost or how relatively few people actually make it to China or into a film, even *Zombie Bloodbath Part 2*. At seven, most of us haven't often been "put in our place" or given the full litany of what others are convinced we cannot do. Nevertheless, making this kind of list at any age opens up a world of possibilities, and tells the opposition that it hasn't had the last word.

Adair had stumbled onto the phenomenon of the *life list,* a document stating all the things you want to do, see, and learn during the rest of your time on earth. On one level, it's a plan of action, but there is a metaphysical dimension to it as well. "There's power in putting what you want on paper: it sets your intention, makes it concrete," says life coach Barbara Biziou, author of *The Joy of Ritual.* "A life list is also a direct communication with Spirit because it's a way to put out clear energy. You can only get help when you're clear about what you want."

For a lot of people, it helps to see this as a wish list rather than a decades-long version of the daily to-do list, which can be a treacherous taskmaster. The idea is to help you rise above the ordinary—"Turn in the report, pick up the dry cleaning"—and not just add "Jump out of an airplane" as another must-do hanging over your head. To write your life list, give yourself a little time and start jotting down whatever comes up.

123

Most experts suggest listing one hundred objectives. They can be monumental (climb Everest) or seemingly frivolous (wear skirts more often). The only rule is to refrain from judgment and just write. This is not a legal document or a sworn oath; you're free to make changes whenever you like and add other intentions as you tick off those you fulfill. Making the list, however, and referring to it periodically gives you focus at both a conscious and subconscious level. It's this focus that helps your assorted dreams move from pie-in-the-sky to sweet-likelihood-on-earth.

If you've reached midlife, you may find it helpful to make a two-part life list: the conventional one of what you want to do, have, and accomplish going forward, and another of what you've *already* done, acquired, and achieved. What would have been on your life list at eighteen? If you think about it, you have fulfilled many of those ambitions. Seeing in black and white what you've already pulled off is a great boost to believing that you can achieve your latter-day objectives as well.

Refer to your list periodically, at least once a month. Be selective, however, about who else sees it. You'll run into opposition if you show it to people who feel threatened by your vision and determination. Sharing it with friends and family (and even a whole Web-based community on an interactive life-list site) can elicit moral support and possibly practical help. Still, it's better to err on the side of keeping things private than expose your embryonic dreams to jealousy or ridicule.

Is anything off-limits? Can some things be too grandiose or too outrageous? Of course, theoretically, but I doubt that you'll waste the time and ink to put those on your list. The more common error is to leave something out that *could* be done but that seems so far beyond us that we write it off as being over the top. Remember: "If you can conceive it"—I'm paraphrasing Napoleon Hill's classic *Think and Grow Rich*—"you can achieve it." Just be sure you can indeed form the conception. If you know deep within yourself that you can do something, who's to say you can't?

Lucky Charm

*Take a couple of pages in the notebook where
you've been keeping your serendipity log and write
up a life list. Edit, alter, and elaborate at will.*

30

Detox your body

It makes sense to keep as many toxins
out of our bodies as we can,
and to assist the various organs and systems
charged with detoxification
to better perform this important job.

Everything we do on earth requires our bodies' participation. When they feel light and free, we tend to feel balanced emotionally, mentally, and spiritually, too. In order for a body to feel this good, nourishment and detoxification need to be working in harmony: you take in what you need (air, water, food), use it for myriad physiological processes, and release the excess.

Activities as basic as breathing and exercise create waste materials that have to be dealt with, and the exigencies of modern life—ongoing stress, exposure to chemical contaminants, foods that are less than ideal—markedly increase the toxic load. Therefore, it makes sense to keep as many toxins out of our bodies as we can, and to assist the various organs and systems charged with detoxification to better perform this important job. To do this, try:

A Dozen Detoxers for Your Body

1. Drink plenty of water. Keep yourself hydrated throughout the day. Drink room-temperature water or hot water with lemon, so your 98.6-degree body won't have to warm up ice water. Herbal teas count as water, as do fresh vegetable juices and the fermented herbal beverage *kombucha,* which provides lots of good bacteria for optimal digestion.

2. Cut out or cut back on alcohol and caffeine. When doctors give the green light for "moderate alcohol consumption," they mean one glass of wine, one beer, or one shot of liquor daily for women, twice that for men. If you consume more than this, consider cutting back. Moreover, in yogic teachings alcohol is seen as *tamasic,* leading to feelings of heaviness and lethargy—the opposite of what's called for in maintaining a charmed life.

Caffeine has been linked to stress and anxiety, insomnia, heart disease, fibromyalgia, and a host of other problems. Keep your intake reasonable. If you decide to eliminate it altogether, avoid the withdrawal headache by doing this slowly: go from coffee to black tea to green tea to caffeine-free herbal teas and the delicious brewed coffee substitute Teeccino. After three to four weeks, your stress hormone levels, stimulated by caffeine, will normalize and you should feel post-coffee fabulous without the coffee.

Whatever your beverage choice, you may want to forgo artificial sweeteners. Agave nectar is a light liquid sweetener, low on the glycemic index, that comes from a cactus plant. And many tea and coffee drinkers are sold on the calorie-free herbal sweetener stevia. (I think it has a funny taste, but I'd use it before the fake stuff.)

3. *Eat organically grown food whenever possible.* It's good for the planet, for conscientious small farmers, and for lightening the toxic load on your one and only body. If you eat animal products, be sure these are organic, because pesticide residues concentrate and magnify in animal tissue. As for produce, do your best to choose organic when you're shopping for those fruits and vegetables that tend to be the most heavily sprayed: grapes (and raisins), peanuts (and peanut butter), apples (and applesauce), berries, broccoli, leafy greens, celery, cucumbers, and peaches. Frequenting farmers' markets, joining a food co-op or CSA (community-supported agriculture—you buy a share for the season in a small, organic farm), and growing a garden are all ways to keep the costs down.

4. *Consume plenty of fiber.* Give your colon some help by eating plenty of foods that act as an "intestinal broom." Blackberries, pears, apples, peas, sweet potatoes, almonds, dried beans, and oatmeal all contain laudable amounts of healthy fiber. The fiber that helps most with "regularity" is found in whole wheat and wheat bran, whole rye (think Scandinavian flat bread), brown rice, figs and prunes, and ground flaxseed. If you're not used to eating fiber-rich foods, increase your intake gradually so your digestive system can adapt.

127

5. Scrape your tongue in the morning. Every morning before you eat or drink anything (or kiss anybody, for that matter), use a little metal scraper you can find in the dental-care aisle of a drug or health-food store and scrape the "sweater" off your tongue. In Ayurvedic medicine, this coating is called *ama,* metabolic debris that is meant to leave your body. Removing this stuff is also a simple, effective way to ensure nice breath.

6. Do dry-skin brushing. More than a pound of waste is expelled through the skin every day. Help it do its job by brushing yourself rosy with a special dry-skin brush before you bathe or shower. The brush, which you'll find at a natural-foods store or good pharmacy, comes with a long, removable handle so you can reach your back. Start with the soles of your feet and brush quickly and lightly, working up your body using long strokes on your arms and legs, brushing in the direction of your heart, and round motions on your torso. Skip your face; the brush is too rough for facial skin. Expect the procedure to remove dead skin cells, rev up lymph and blood circulation, strengthen immunity, and possibly even help to keep cellulite at bay.

7. Sweat. Another way to help your skin help you stay healthy is to perspire. Do this through vigorous exercise, steam baths or saunas, Bikram yoga (done in a very hot room), and the hydrotherapeutic technique of hot-and-cold showers. To do this, alternate five minutes in a steamy shower with thirty seconds of cold water; repeat the cycle three times; then get under the covers for half an hour.

My husband does this whenever he feels that he's coming down with something, and in thirteen years I've known him to get only two full-blown colds.

8. Enjoy a massage. In addition to promoting relaxation and boosting immunity, massage improves blood circulation and the flow of lymphatic fluid in the body. If it seems like an expensive indulgence, check for massage-therapy schools in your area where professional-level treatments are low in cost but still long on benefits.

9. Use your cell phone less. In addition to anecdotal evidence—complaints of fatigue, headaches, irritability, and sleeplessness among those who use mobile phones for long periods—a growing body of research suggests that repeated, long-term exposure to electromagnetic-field radiation from cell phones may cause brain-tissue damage. To be on the safe side, don't give up your land line and let that be the number you give people. Use the cell for short calls only (if you need incentive, reduce the number of minutes on your plan), and charge your phone somewhere other than your bedroom.

10. Purify your indoor air. Use only natural cleaning products and paints low on volatile organic compounds (Sherwin-Williams's Harmony line or Benjamin Moore's Aura). Get rid of plastic and vinyl products that can emit potentially carcinogenic gases. (You might start by replacing your vinyl shower curtain with a cloth one.) When it's time for a new mattress or bedclothes, invest in those made from organic materials. If you burn candles, choose those made of beeswax, soy, or palm oil with cotton wicks. Have houseplants to help clean the air; among the best are bamboo, Chinese evergreen, English ivy, Gerbera daisy, mother-in-law's tongue, and peace lily.

Minimize electromagnetic-field radiation by unplugging appliances that aren't in use, especially anything with a box that plugs into the outlet. Use an alarm clock with a battery, not a plug, and put it at least six feet from your bed. (Added bonus: you'll get *up* in the morning rather than hit the snooze button.) Keep your furnace filter clean, and have your home's air ducts irrigated every couple of years.

11. Do deep breathing. Now that your air is clean, take a deep breath. In fact, take several. Even a few slow, deep breaths can markedly increase your oxygen intake. Try yoga's three-part breath: Inhale through your nose, first expanding your abdomen (part 1), then your diaphragm (part 2), and finally your chest (part 3). Then exhale and continue with the next round. When you get used to doing this, try to make your exhale a little longer than your inhale, imagining yourself pushing all the stale air out of your lungs. And when you can do your deep breathing in a large park, in the woods, or at the beach—well, that's all the better.

12. Juice-fast for a day or two or three. Fasting is a time-honored therapy, allowing the body to devote energy otherwise used for digestion to detoxification, cleansing, and healing. Fasting only on water requires competent professional supervision, but a healthy person can do a short juice

fast at home, consuming three to five glasses of freshly extracted vegetable and fruit juice daily and drinking water
and caffeine-free herbal teas at will. If you're drinking fruit
juice alone, dilute it with pure water to reduce the sugar
content. Juice combinations that fasters enjoy are apple/
celery, carrot/spinach/parsley, apple/kale/ginger, and—
my favorite—tomato/arugula/lemon. But use your imagination. Boost the efficacy of your fast by employing other
suggestions from the "detox dozen" list during this time,
and be sure to get plenty of rest.

Lucky Charm

*Do something today
to help your body cleanse and heal.*

31

Detox your life

Feed your mind and heart
uplifting ideas and images.

Just as the body can be overwhelmed by environmental pollutants and dietary indiscretions, life in general can feel toxic, sluggish, and blocked if you don't step back from time to time to detoxify your mind and soul. A mental/spiritual detox is indicated when you're in a chronic bad mood, very little seems exciting, or you're tired in a way that's different from how you feel after a long hike or a productive day's work. It's a weariness that makes you want to say, "What's the use?"

You certainly want to feed your body good food and pure water and detox it by practicing the suggestions in chapter 30. However, it's just as important to feed your mind and heart uplifting ideas and images. When you do this, it clears out the debris of difficulties, disappointments, and unpleasant encounters.

A Dozen Detoxers for Your Life

1. Limit your news exposure. Ingest only as much of the national and world news as you can tolerate each day before it starts to weigh on you. Of course you want to be informed, but be informed only to the point of healthy anger. Becoming passionately pissed off about something can motivate you to take action to make things better. If you get to fear or depression, you'll still be informed but too sad, frightened, and immobilized to act on the information.

2. *Get a change of scenery.* Taking a vacation is great, but you can also get a change of scenery in a garden or a quiet church. Or by taking a different route to the mall and going to stores you don't tend to frequent when you get there. Visiting a friend's home for the first time or trying a new restaurant provides a whole new palette to experience. Even tending to an errand at a different post office or bank branch can be refreshing.

3. *Be around happy people.* They'll listen, within reason, to a tale of woe, but won't commiserate or come down to that level. Instead they'll suggest ways to change things for the better. Emulate them. My most positive friend is always saying, "Have your best day ever!" My immediate mental response used to be: "Fat chance. The odds that out of all the days in my life, this will be the best are about thirty thousand to one." Now I just think, "Cool. This could be my best day ever."

4. *Spend time with animals.* It's relaxing to observe and commune with a dog, cat, horse, gerbil, or even the birds and squirrels outside. They're social like we are, and they accept us as we come. If there is a furred or feathered

member of your family already, you're ahead of the game. Myriad studies show that people with pets have lower blood pressure and lower triglyceride levels than people in humans-only households; some even suggest that sharing your home with someone who'll teach you the importance of a good meal and a good romp may prolong your life.

If living with an animal isn't practical for you, befriend your friends' and neighbors' nonhuman companions. Visit an animal sanctuary and become the virtual adoptive parent of a rescued goose or a quick-witted pig. Or just sit on your back porch and make friends at a distance with the regular visitors to your own yard. After all, you guys share an ecosystem.

5. Be moved by culture. I love live theater, especially musicals. It's worth two hours in the half-price ticket line to sit there in the dark getting thrill bumps during the overture, again when the star comes onstage, and every time they play the refrain of the show's most moving song. Whatever gives you thrill bumps—Beethoven, Emily Dickinson, Turner Classic Movies—needs to be in your life on a regular basis. Every time you're thrilled, you're detoxing the ho-hum.

6. Get some genuine recreation. This is real play, unencumbered by an emphasis on winning and losing, how skilled you are at this game or that sport, and how you look in a tennis skirt. If your recreation is window-shopping, watching the Food Channel, or spending hours in an antique store looking for one perfect postcard, this is good.

135

Don't let anybody tell you that you ought to give up what gives you pleasure and take up what gives them pleasure.

7. Do work you love. Whether on the job or after hours, doing work you love detoxes a spirit that's fed up with work it's not suited to. Even if there's not much to love in your current job, try to devote a portion of each day to some work you really enjoy. It makes tending to the rest of what needs doing far more palatable.

8. Delegate the drudgery when you can. Like beauty, drudgery is in the eye of the beholder. While I'm not crazy about cleaning the toilet or scraping gunk out of the fridge with elbow grease and baking soda, I can do these chores and when they're over, they're over; I feel fine. Not so with detail work in my office. Too much of that and my spirit goes flat, telling me I can use some help. What can you delegate to a family member, a subordinate, or some bright, affordable person who's looking this minute for your classified ad?

9. Laugh uproariously. There's not only magic in every moment; there's irony, too—something to laugh about. Find it: tell jokes; read humor books; look at the funny cards in the store and send one to a sourpuss you know. Laughter offsets the seriousness of life, aids relaxation and healing, and puts you in a positive frame of mind.

10. Partake of inspiration. Inspiration is, literally, a breath of fresh air. Maintain your inspiration level at least at full, and ideally at brimming over. Keep little books like this one in your desk drawer and glove compartment, on your nightstand and end tables. If the saying on a magnet moves you, find a place for it on your refrigerator door. If you see a quotation or read a piece of scripture and your hearts skips a beat at its beauty and its wisdom, copy it in your journal or tape it to your bathroom mirror until you commit it to memory.

11. Organize something (and, ultimately, everything). It's a stretch to see the wonder in your life when the papers on your desk are covering it up. If you tend to be disorganized (I admit to being in that camp), you have probably come to realize that decluttering is not a onetime project, or even something as periodic as "spring cleaning." It's a daily enterprise, made easier if you adopt certain good habits such as setting aside the last half hour of the workday to put things in order at the office, and getting the dishes done every evening *before* you turn on the TV.

If clutter is a big problem and you've been unable to come up with a system that keeps it under control (or to stick with the system you've decided on), consider engaging the services of a professional organizer. Some people just have the knack. Chances are you can find an organizer online whose rates are low but who can revolutionize the state of your desk, your closets, and (maybe) your life.

12. Do a house blessing or a space-clearing ritual. A ritual does for psychic space what getting organized does for physical space: clears it out and gives it back to you fresh and new. Although recommended for a new residence or if there has been exceptional sadness, anger, or discord in

137

the home, there's never a wrong time to do a little invisible housekeeping. A lot of people swear by "smudging with sage." You buy a big bunch of sage, called a *frond,* at a health-food store or metaphysical bookshop, light it, and carry it through your house, letting the fragrant smoke float into every nook and corner, and holding the intention that it is clearing things out. This is supposed to get rid of bad energy, and I always feel that it does.

If you're not quite that ritualistic, Rev. Laurie Sue Brockway, author of *A Goddess Is a Girl's Best Friend,* suggests something as simple as dancing the negativity away: "You can easily clear unpleasant energies from a home by replacing them with energies of a higher vibration. Any time your home is feeling heavy or dark, turn on some spicy music that makes you want to dance. Then waltz, cha-cha, or hip-hop into every room of the house, filling it with joy as you imagine a new radiance filling your abode. Repeat as needed and feel free to use a new tune each time."

Lucky Charm

Honor your mental/emotional/spiritual self by refusing to believe that it's supposed to "suck up" all kinds of unpleasantness and negativity. Detox daily by doing away with a little excess and bringing on a little joie de vivre.

32

Fill your life with beauty

Even when you're going through
a difficult spell, you know that life
can at least be pretty.
You owe yourself that.

The place I've visited that was most unlike what I'm used to and most extraordinary to remember is Tibet. In a memory so exotic I can hardly believe it's really mine, a worker from the Save the Children office in Lhasa invited my daughter and me with him on a trip into the interior of the country to visit the nomads, yak herders whose way of life has changed very little over time. They live in tents and move every few months, following the sparse vegetation that feeds their herd.

One family—the husband was the head of a nomadic group and they had the biggest tent—invited us in for tea. This was yak-butter tea, definitely an acquired taste and an acquired smell. It was served, however, in delicate china cups, painted with flowers that don't grow in the Himalayas. I don't know where those cups came from—gifts from a missionary to someone's grandmother? Barter with an adventurer seventy years ago? However these English cups and saucers came into this family's hands, they had survived their share of rugged travel to be proffered for the delight of visitors and the pride of our hosts.

That day in a tent on the roof of the world, those cups were my teachers. They taught me that beauty is not an insignificant extra or a luxury one can do without. Beauty is a human need. It transcends language and culture, speaking straight to the soul and requiring no translation.

When you live a charmed life, your very existence is drenched in beauty. You seek it out in nature and galleries, in fabric colors and china patterns. You see it where someone else could miss it—the antique street lamps on a single block, the spider web bejeweled with raindrops, the lace tablecloth on the bottom of a pile at the thrift store. You wake up to beauty in the way you've outfitted your bedroom and what you focus on outside when you open your shades. You choose from beautiful clothes in your closet and beautiful fruits for your cereal. You take a beautiful route to work and spend the day in a beautiful office (or as beautiful as policy allows). Even when you're going through a difficult spell, you know that life can at least be pretty. You owe yourself that.

Having fresh flowers around is one way to put a patch of beauty just about anywhere. In his delight of a book, *Letting the Lotus Bloom: The Expression of Soul Through Flowers,* Kevin Joel Kelly writes: "Flowers are voiceless companions who continually share their wisdom and enhance our days. They shout for us to wake up when we are sleepy-eyed, ignoring the beauty of life. They teach us about the fragility of life and they tempt us to indulge in the pleasure of this moment." I think this is why flowers are traditional at funerals: they lift spirits in the darkest times. And we send them to sick people because we know that beauty is healing. They're preventive medicine, too, and we can all use a regular prescription.

So what can you do besides arrange flowers in a vase to make your life lovely? Sew new curtains? Plant a garden? Hang a print? Clean things up so the beauty that's already in your home can shine? One way to get started is to remove anything you come across that's ugly (or broken or useless). Get it out of your life, or at least out of your field of vision—even if it was a gift. No one should cause you to have to live with something that brings you down, even a little bit, every time you see it. Of course if you live with someone who thinks this object is the cat's meow, you won't be able to banish it forevermore, but maybe you can move it to a room where your truelove or your darling child can enjoy it and you can forget, most of the time, that it's there.

141

Even things that everyone agrees on can seem old and dull if you've looked at them every day for years, so set up a rotation system. Keep some artwork, small pieces of furniture, rugs, and so forth in storage so you can alternate them annually or every six months. With a fresh eye, you'll remember why you loved each piece when you bought it.

Concentrating on one object of beauty at a time trains your eye and your soul to look for beauty everywhere and have it register when you come upon it. To that end, play a little game by selecting a "beautiful item of the week." No one else has to know you're doing this. Decide that the small bronze statue of Icarus just before his wings melted when he flew too close to the sun will be the object to which you'll pay special attention this week. You'll spend a little time with it, looking at it from every angle, touching it to find the beauty with your fingers as well as your eyes. Next week you might choose for the honor a framed sunset photograph you took on vacation last summer. And the week after that it might be a particular houseplant whose leaves are the most exquisite combination of dusky pink and earthy green.

A Native American prayer says, "Beauty behind me, beauty before me, beauty beyond me, beauty beneath me." Look for it everywhere.

Lucky Charm

Before this day is over, do one small thing that makes your life prettier. Then, before you go to sleep tonight, give yourself the suggestion that doing this daily is going to become a habit.

33

Do the cosmic two-step

Ask knowing that you already have it.
Accepting that it's in the works,
you don't have to do a thing besides
follow up on whatever
strokes of genius come to you.

There is an efficient two-step process for bringing what you want into being. Used properly, this will hasten the transformation of dreams into reality, provided, of course, that those particular dreams are for your highest good. OK, here's the formula:

1. Ask for what you want.
2. Let it go.

Seems simple enough. But we're human. We can complicate anything.

To make it easy, let's break it down: *Ask for what you want.* It seems odd that we need to ask for anything when God or the universe must already know what we want. Like so much spiritual practice, though, God doesn't need it; we do. When we ask for what we want, we bring it into focus. It's no longer an airy-fairy "It might be nice if . . ." kind of daydreaming; this is now something to which we've staked a claim.

A classic image of the power of asking comes from the film version of *Gone with the Wind*. Scarlett O'Hara—traumatized by war, delirious with grief, the world she knew decimated—is frantically digging in the sweet potato field for something left from last year's crop. Half starved and unable to feed those in her care, she screams at heaven, "As God is my witness, I'll never be hungry again!" Now, that's some first-rate asking. While we sit watching the film with our popcorn, we're witnessing the ultimate affirmative prayer.

Rent the movie if you haven't seen it in a while, and pay close attention to that scene. Your need does not have to be this acute, your asking does not have to be this dramatic, and chances are there won't be background music, but you want to ask with the same focused, single-minded intent. Think of something you asked for or prayed for that didn't turn out. Now think of Scarlett. How did your asking compare with hers? I rest my case.

When you ask, you have to ask knowing that you already have it. This isn't weirdo stuff; even Jesus said, "All things whatsoever ye pray and ask for, believe that ye have received them, and ye shall have them." Accepting that it's in the works, you don't have to do a thing besides follow up on whatever strokes of genius come to you ("Make a dress out of draperies" . . . "Visit Rhett in prison").

Let it go. This is step two. It's harder than step one. While we are responsible for taking the action that is ours to take (doing the footwork, following through on the task at hand and those highly intelligent inklings), we have to let go of the rest. Otherwise, we

144

overthink, ruminating to our peril. "Is this the right thing after all? Do I deserve it? Will people still like me after I get this?" Or we doubt the viability of this thing we've done such a good job of asking for: "On second thought, this is a lot to expect. Maybe in this economy I should really rethink it. I got what I asked for last time; I wonder if I should wait awhile before I ask again." Let it go, let it go, let it go.

What can happen? You'll either get it (that's great), or you won't (because this is not the time or there's something better in store), or you'll get it in a different form from what you'd thought. This different-form thing happens all the time.

When *Creating a Charmed Life* was new, I wanted so much to be invited onto *The Oprah Winfrey Show* with it. I asked. (Believe me: like Scarlett, I asked!) And lo and behold, one of the producers called. She said, "We want you and *Shelter for the Spirit*." But that was my previous book, going on two years old. "No, you don't understand," I explained, "the new book is *Creating a Charmed Life*." There was a silence that may have lasted three seconds but felt like three years. "We *want*," she emphasized, "*Shelter for the Spirit*." This time I really heard her. I said, "Yes, certainly" to the producer, and inside, "Thank you, God." The segment turned out beautifully, and a few years later, with yet another book, *Lit from Within,* I was on the show again—not with the book I'd pasted to my vision board, but *two books* total. Who's complaining?

I know of course, as you do, that not everything we ask for is in the bonus category like getting to be on an amazing TV show. Sometimes we ask for a loved one to pull through an illness and they don't, or we ask to keep our job during mass layoffs and we lose it like everybody else. Sometimes we ask to get pregnant or receive a promising phone call or get some sign that everything is going to be OK, and all we get is a big fat negative on the pregnancy test, a "You have zero messages" on the voice mail, and no signs about anything showing up anywhere. This is when the universe appears to have taken an indefinite leave of absence. Mystics, men and women who have had direct experience of the Divine, call it "the dark night of the soul." Nobody likes it, not even mystics. The two-step choreography doesn't change, however: ask for what you want, and let it go.

And if the outcome is other than what you've asked for, no matter how skillfully you asked and how assiduously you left it alone, know even then that nothing is lost. The energy of your asking and the grace of your detachment still have power, and they're still at work to bring you closer to your destiny, despite the detour. See a life growing up around you that is charmed in both its joy and its sorrow. Observe your own soul and your own character growing more flexible and understanding, more beautiful and more brilliant. This two-step is simple, and simply spectacular.

146

Lucky Charm

What do you want today? Ask for it.
Then let it go and await instructions.

Indulge in your simplest pleasure

Your simplest pleasure is basic,
easy to access, cheap,
and independent of any other person.

The day had been, to put it generously, uninspiring. I'd been traveling and had failed to perform several key tasks the previous day,
leaving myself unprepared for what was expected of me on the current one. I traded the gym, meditation, and the newspaper for a
mad game of catch-up, interspersed with apologies to everyone I'd
stood up or let down.

By evening, I was spent. I barely had the energy to draw a bath
and sink into the bubbly tub, but when I did I heard myself saying,
"This is hands-down the best thing that's happened today." I knew
in a flash what had just transpired: I'd identified, and was indulging
in, my simplest pleasure.

I have never been disappointed by a hot bath. Each one is intensely satisfying and so luxurious I wonder why it doesn't cost
more than a few cents on the water bill. Candles and lavender
oil and warmed towels, nice when they're available, are mere

embellishments. The bath itself is an unparalleled delight without any pomp and circumstance. That's what makes it my simplest pleasure: it's basic, easy to access, cheap, and not dependent on any other person.

Your simplest pleasure, whatever it may be, meets these criteria, too. What makes this particular activity stand out from the many other things that you enjoy is that you can get it just about any time you want and without expending a lot of effort. The acid test for a simplest pleasure is an affirmative answer to the following question: "Can I avail myself of this pleasure within the next twenty-four hours without having to get permission, make arrangements, or spend more money than I could painlessly part with several times a week?" If yes, go for it.

148

Think carefully of what your *simplest* pleasure is. For example, "sitting in front of a crackling fire" can be your simplest pleasure, but only if you have easy access to a wood-burning hearth. If you don't, it's still lovely, but having to drive to your mom's house or to that hotel downtown with the great fireplace in the lobby would probably keep it from qualifying as "simplest."

Here are some simplest pleasures friends and life-coaching clients have shared with me. Perhaps you'll recognize yours on this list, or a kindred joy that brings yours to mind.

- ❀ "Dancing. I love to go out dancing, but I can get that rush of happy feelings just dancing by myself in the living room."
- ❀ "Being in my garden. The weather doesn't matter."
- ❀ "Watching one of the comedy DVDs I collect. I can know every line in the movie and still laugh like crazy."

❀ "Knitting. I carry my knitting with me all the time. I've finally stopped feeling insulted when people ask if I'm pregnant. A lot of them seem to think that expecting a baby is the only reason to knit. They're so wrong."

❀ "Listening to smooth jazz."

❀ "Looking through old photo albums and appreciating what a great life I've had (and am having)."

❀ "Sitting with a cup of tea. It can be English breakfast first thing in the morning, jasmine in the afternoon, chamomile before bed. Just put a teacup in front of me and I relax."

❀ "Reading the mystical poets—Rumi, Blake, Wordsworth, Whitman. I just can't get enough."

❀ "Doing yoga postures. I learned yoga a long time ago before it got so athletic. The yoga I do gets me from wherever I start, even if that's stressed out and worn out, to a place of peace in nothing flat."

❀ "Cuddling with my husband."

OK, that last one involves another person, but if he's also a cuddler, it may be his simplest pleasure, too.

Lucky Charm
❀

Identify your simplest pleasure,
and indulge in it within the next
twenty-four hours.

149

35

Take train trips and road trips

Down here at ground level
you'll discover America—
and maybe even yourself.

Flying has become an odd default. When I do it I fall into the drill like everyone else: dutifully arriving two hours in advance, disrobing for security to whatever extent is necessary, bringing my lunch (no liquids, of course) and a blanket and pillow. It's almost like camping. Coach seats in most planes are so close together that the last time I flew I got a bruised kneecap when the woman in the seat ahead of me abruptly reclined. (There may not be many meals served in the sky these days, but the trays are still in the seatbacks, and on direct impact they're lethal.)

I understand that, barring a blizzard in the Midwest or lightning in Atlanta, flying is the fastest way to get places, and often it's the only viable option. If alternatives are available, however, you owe it to yourself to check them out.

Taking the train is a captivating experience, and if you've never done it, you're missing something that is both affordable and sublime. It's also the most environmentally sound means of travel short of a bicycle or your own two feet. There's romance to the railroad, a combination of classic movie scenes remembered and timeless Americana outside the windows from sea to shining sea. As a passenger, you get to snuggle into a big, comfy seat, and if you're one for talking to strangers, you'll find your fellow riders intriguing.

On one trip, I met a businesswoman from Chicago who told me that when the pressures pile up, she books a ticket with sleeper accommodations to and from Washington, D.C. She spends the first night unwinding in her private cocoon and devotes the next day to exploring her favorite capital bookshops and dining on international cuisine in the Adams Morgan district. By evening, she's ready to be lulled to sleep once more by the comforting motion of the car and the soothing hum of the locomotive as she heads homeward.

If you're taking a long trip and you spring for a sleeping room as she does, you'll get your own little den with practical accoutrements that pull out of the wall: the bed, the basin, the toilet—even an easy chair for reading, working, and gazing at the landscape as it changes like a slide show. The sleeper car is an engineering tour de force that offers a degree of coziness not readily experienced elsewhere.

Opportunities for going by train are limited in many parts of the country, but if there is an Amtrak station near where you live, that train goes somewhere and you owe yourself the pleasure of taking it. Especially if you're someone who's always rushing and feeling behind schedule, traveling by train—once a year or even once in a lifetime—tells the despot time that you're taking control of yours and investing it as you please.

Besides, when you go by rail, you arrive at your actual destination, not in some erstwhile cornfield forty miles out, where so many airports are located. And should you have a layover, you're in the middle of the city, so you can actually wander around Boston or St. Louis. And for the rest of your life, when someone asks if you've been there, you never have to say, "Not really—I was just at the airport."

Another option for land-based adventuring, road trips have their own quirky joys, especially if you get off the scenery-starved interstate and take some state and county highways. This is where you'll discover towns that will make you think you're in Mayberry or Grover's Corners or Bedford Falls. You can dine in diners replete with home cooking and nostalgic charm. You can antique in antique shops that are finds in themselves, and talk with family farmers keen on educating the rest of us about how hard it is to work the land in this day of era-ending competition from corporate agriculture.

When you drive, provided you're willing to take appropriate detours and make stops along the way, you'll discover the signature qualities that persist in the various regions of this country, qualities that are muted in more traveled areas by identical fast-food places and warehouse stores. Down here at ground level, you'll discover America—and maybe even yourself.

Writer and theater director Leonard Peters is a native New Yorker who viewed the rest of the United States as a second-class suburb of Manhattan until he took the opportunity to drive cross-country to deliver a car for a friend. Peters headed west over the George Washington Bridge, determined to keep an open mind. He

153

returned after six weeks a changed man, and he is documenting his experience in a book, *Love and Awakening in America*. "America," he says, "is an awe-inspiring, breathtaking, and beautiful country like no other I have ever seen. New York City is as unique and special to me as ever, but I see it now as a part of a much more majestic and magnificent landscape."

These are charmed-life sentiments if I ever heard them.

Lucky Charm

Go to the Amtrak Web site and see where the trains are. Or haul out your atlas and gas up your hybrid (until the great day when we can plug in our electric cars). Alternatively, check out the bus so someone else can drive. Then take a little trip and expect, as with life itself, that getting there really will be half the fun.

154

36

Claim a cafe

You need a cafe the same way you need a best
friend, a favorite color, work that you're proud
of, and a hobby you love.

Natalie Goldberg is a wonderful writer's writer who encouraged
me years ago in books such as *Wild Mind* and *Writing Down the
Bones* to ply my trade at a well-placed table in a compatible cafe.
I use my home office for research and editing, coaching and radio
interviews, and the endless marketing tasks and clerical details that
are a component of any business. To meet the muse, however, I go
to a coffee shop.

I've come to see that claiming a cafe is not the sole province
of writers and students. We all need a place to go where we can be
alone with company, where the waiter or barista knows our order
in advance, and where a certain corner is, more often than not,
ours. Although there is much to be said for both pure solitude and
the companionship of family and friends, a special way of being is
"out and about but unencumbered." At your cafe, you get the energy of the people around you, inspiration from a woman's locket

or a little boy's lollypop, and heartening freedom from undone chores, a ringing doorbell, and, if you leave your cell phone at home and don't sign up for Wi-Fi, other people's demands on your time.

Depending on your circumstances, you may spend a few hours a day at your cafe as I do, or twenty minutes before work skimming the paper and gearing up for the day. Maybe Saturday mornings when the kids are at ballet can be your time to drink something foamy and either read something enthralling or write something profound, whether for public viewing or private pleasure. Whatever the particulars, this is a personal retreat to soothe your soul and stoke your creativity.

If your choice of cafes is limited and you have to travel to get to yours, have a backup: a picnic table, a library, or a bookstore with a seating area from which no one will rouse you mid-thought. Why go to the trouble? You need a cafe (or surrogate) for the same reason you need a best friend, a favorite color, work that you're proud of, and a hobby you love. These give you dimension and definition. So does having a place to go where you can access your genius for the price of a ginger tea and an oatmeal cookie.

Lucky Charm

Check out cafes near your home and office.
Do you need tranquility or stimulation?
A plug for your laptop, or pottery mugs and
perfect scones? When you find this second home,
let it feed you in all sorts of ways.

37

Be completely, utterly yourself

What is so priceless
about being the selves
we were created to grow into
is that it's impossible
to do it wrong.

There is no one with more promise than a ten-year-old girl. She is convinced that she can do anything and that no one can stop her. Her heart is as big as the sky, and when she believes in something, she is tireless in her advocacy. If ten-year-old girls ran the world, everybody would be nice, everything within human control would be fair, and anyone who wanted could have a horse.

Then something happens. Somewhere between eleven and fourteen, hormones surge, self-confidence often plummets, and what other people think becomes more important than that plan to be an astronaut or a diplomat. That's when we tell the adolescent that all she has to do is be herself. Even though we know she may not be able to follow through on this, we want desperately for her to try. If we're honest, we know we're still trying to do this ourselves, and that when we succeed we're over the moon.

As adults we know that anyone of any age who is completely and utterly herself in every situation has carte blanche on the best that life offers. These women (and men) never apologize for who they are or take on the persona of someone else. They know that today they're fine just as they are, even if they're working to change a habit or improve a skill. They don't expect themselves to be perfect, only charmingly, quirkily, and engagingly one of a kind.

Camille Maurine is a colleague of mine (she wrote *Meditation Secrets for Women*), but since she's on the West Coast and I'm on the East, we'd never met. It happened that we were both to be in London at the same time, and we planned a rendezvous at Top Floor, a city-view restaurant in the Peter Jones department store. I arrived first with another friend and assumed we'd know Camille from her picture. When she showed up, it was obvious we'd have known her with no prior likeness to go on. She strode off the escalator, raised her arms overhead in a V shape, and announced, "I'm here!"

Indeed she was: a woman who had no fear whatsoever about making an entrance. She came into that restaurant the way a diva would walk onto an opera stage, fully confident in her knowledge that she would give people more in sharing her gifts than she would take from their ample appreciation. This woman I didn't know yet was so comfortable with herself that it seemed a good bet that I'd be comfortable with her, too.

This was Camille being Camille. Someone else could have entered quietly, discreetly scanning tables until she found ours, and been every bit as true to herself and every bit as striking in a different way. That's what is so priceless about being the selves we were created to grow into: it's impossible to do it wrong. The only way to fail is to deny that self.

When I asked Camille for permission to tell this story, she didn't remember the escalator *ta-dah,* but she didn't doubt it either. "I was just so excited to meet you, to be in London, to see what life would bring," she wrote. "So it's true: in that moment, I was being myself. To have acted otherwise would have been inauthentic, stultifying, and unhealthy."

It's the same for us anytime we're tempted to impersonate someone we believe might be more acceptable. While an accomplished actress can act like somebody else, no one can live as somebody else. This is not to imply that being yourself is always easy. Say you're in a group in which everyone holds a political or social view that you oppose. You don't necessarily have to volunteer your position (in many cases, it's probably wise not to), but if you hide it or pretend to have a different viewpoint just to fit in, you deny the woman you've invested so much in becoming. In these cases, stick with topics you can agree on if possible. If a bone of contention turns up in the conversational stew, balance conviction and civility. In other words, stand by your guns but don't shoot anybody. Say something like, "If I didn't know what terrific arguments you guys could come up with, I'd actually try to make a point for the opposition."

It's more serious, of course, if you're in a marriage or other committed relationship in which you can't be yourself, possibly because you pretended early on to be somebody different and landed yourself a partner who was looking for the woman in your charade.

159

Even in a situation like this, however, your true self is going to find a way to express if all Hades breaks loose. To help her do that (without the Hades part), consider the following:

Ways to Be Yourself

(when that seems like too much, not enough, or simply unwelcome)

Know who you are and what you like. Tweens and young teens get encouragement for this with annotated diaries and magazine questionnaires that ask, "What are my favorite things to do on a Saturday morning?" and "If I could have a party and invite anyone, living or dead, who would be on my guest list?" As adults we find ourselves too busy for such egocentric cerebration, but a little of it does have a place. What do *you* like doing on Saturday before noon? Who would *you* invite to your party?

Refuse to apologize for your preferences. I've never met a documentary film I didn't like, and William has been known to comment that I would go to any documentary (as if there's something wrong with that). Then I say, "Why, yes, I would. I know myself very well, and obviously you do, too."

Follow through on heart tugs. When something is meaningful to you, follow through, regardless of how it looks to others or to the more circumscribed part of your own personality. If you feel moved to have a conversation with a homeless person or organize a fund-raiser for a crisis in a country you hadn't heard of till yesterday, converse and organize.

Follow up on your interests. If you want to collect ceramic bunnies, or take up belly dancing, or get a master's degree in some field that seems to have nothing to do with your BA or your life up to now, you are fully entitled to do this. The more of your own interests you pursue, the more fully you come into your own.

Decorate (and dress) to express. We covered clothes in chapter 13. Your home, as well as your wardrobe, should tell the world something about who you are and what you value. The colors, style of furniture, the family pictures and personal memorabilia on display all say something— ideally, "Hello, world. This is who I am!" or, if you live with other people, "This is who we are!"

Don't ask for permission or look for approval. No one else can tell you how to be yourself, and some people may be threatened by it. Although anyone who truly loves you loves your authentic self, even they will never be quite as tickled by her full presence as you are. That's only natural. Show your authentic self anyway, both for your own benefit and to model for others that they can be completely, utterly themselves, too.

Have opinions, be ready to change them, and be OK if you're proven wrong. You are entitled to think what you think and believe what you believe. You are also entitled to change your mind. And if you come to learn that something you thought or believed was about as far off base as it could get without leaving the ballpark, be ready to say, "Imagine that! I stand corrected."

Should you fail to gather the considerable courage to be completely, utterly yourself early on, you'll find that midlife makes it easier. Remember that ten-year-old you once were? You'll get her back at fifty or so, complete with matured aspirations and a renewed knowledge of what it is you came here to do that you haven't done yet. It is possible to deny your true self even at this stage, but it's so uncomfortable, you'll either come around or face the bitterness of abandoning the person for whom you're most responsible: you.

Whatever your age and vital statistics, you have a purpose that is uniquely yours. You cannot take on this most essential endeavor while playing a character. Things are designed that way for your own protection: to be sure no one else elbows in on your destiny. So be yourself. There is no one like you.

Lucky Charm

The next time you're tempted
to act like someone you're not—
to tone your flamboyance down
or edge your demureness up—don't.

38

Map the route from bummed to better

Life is too precious
for you to spend one more minute
feeling like overcooked porridge.

People living charmed lives are not immune to down times: they just make those times short. When you cycle through a rough patch, or if you're just feeling bummed, you need to get back as quickly as possible to a place where you can experience joy. The challenge to doing this effortlessly every time is that a down frame of mind is a physical downer, too. When you need extra energy to pull yourself out of a dreary state, chances are you're feeling draggy and lethargic.

Consider this serious and get to work, not because you'd never snap out of the doldrums otherwise, but because life is too precious for you to spend one more minute feeling like overcooked porridge. Start by giving yourself a *doldrums allotment,* aka a *pity party.* Whatever you call it, it is a time-limited period in which you get to play the role of "woe is me." During this time—fifteen minutes to four hours—you can lie around, cry, watch TV, and elaborate on how awful things are to anybody who'll listen. But when the party's over, it's over. Some people do well having their pity party at bedtime—a couple of hours to "get it all out," then a night's sleep and a fresh start.

To make that start, you'll need to take some specific actions. A generic "chin up" won't cut it. The more concrete your action, the more likely you'll do it and the more likely it will help. My top five are pretty fundamental: take a shower; clean up around the house; watch a funny movie; listen to uplifting music; and go out, walk, and breathe.

5 Fundamentals for Bouncing Back

1. Take a shower. I've already shared with you that a long, leisurely bath is my simplest pleasure (chapter 34). Showering serves another purpose. It lets you wash that man (or job or insult or disappointment) right out of your hair while elevating your mood with a citrus-scented scrub or body wash. Practitioners of energy healing also say that when you shower, you're cleansing your subtle "energy body" as well, so you can step out of the shower feeling like a whole new person. Intensify the process by reminding yourself as you shower that you're "coming clean" in every sense of the word. Sing a song that makes you want to believe in yourself—anything from "Amazing Grace" to "What's Love Got to Do with It?" In the shower, being off-key is no problem at all.

2. Clean up around your house. This is not perfection cleaning. It's just straightening a bit, clearing a little clutter, and freshening the stagnant energy that messiness engenders. I will often put right twenty-seven items—pick up a paper clip, hang up a towel, put shoes in the closet, wipe off a counter, and so on. I chose that number because feng shui teaches that moving twenty-seven items (art or pieces of furniture) in your house will change your life. Twenty-seven odds and ends won't change your life, but the very action of it—and the pleasing order you'll see when you finish—can change your mood.

3. Watch a funny movie. Sift through your DVDs or scroll through the pay-per-view listings and find a hilarious movie. Then snuggle up with it and let yourself laugh. If you're a fan of stand-up, an hour with the Comedy Channel works, too. Either way, laughter reduces muscle tension, decreases the level of stress hormones coursing through your body, strengthens your immune system, and improves brain function. No wonder it's fun.

4. Play uplifting music. A study done at Penn State found that moods improve when people listen to *any* music. Traditionally, works of Tchaikovsky, Debussy, Haydn (try the flute quartets), and Chopin, along with those where-do-I-enlist Sousa marches, have been held in high regard as mood elevators. If you respond to lyrics, Broadway show tunes are terrific, especially the one song in every musical that they put there to make you feel that you can do anything. My iPod is an antidepressant with earbuds, packed with songs like "If They Could See Me Now" from *Sweet Charity,* "Some People" from *Gypsy,* "Only

You" from *Starlight Express,* "Hold On" from *The Secret Garden,* and "Make Them Hear You" from *Ragtime.*

5. *Go out, walk, and breathe.* It doesn't take a hike or a power walk to feel a great deal better. Just go outside where the air is moving and walk at a pace that feels right, even if that's slow motion. As you do, pay attention to breathing in and out. "This is an amazing way to get beyond a blue mood," says Manhattan yoga instructor Yetta Freundlich. "When you breathe, you're already exchanging molecules, so it's not such a big step to imagine yourself exchanging fatigue and worry for strength and a powerful attitude."

There are dozens of other maneuvers you can instigate to get yourself from down in the dumps to back in the game. It might be brushing your cat, pulling weeds in the garden, or going to a used bookstore and breathing in the comforting smell of old volumes. It's OK to start with a feel-good action that's small and simple. If going to the gym is too much, try going to the mailbox. Energy begets itself: expend a little and you'll have more.

Lucky Charm

*Decide today that glum moods
need never "run their course." You can
give them a time limit and then start
on the road to a better attitude with something
as simple as taking a steamy shower
or walking around your very own block.*

39

Give peace a chance

Allow circumstances to be
as they are in this moment, and live
in such a way that they'll be different
in the next.

We humans share 98.4 percent of our DNA with the bonobo ape. Bonobos are a fun-loving, vegetarian, pacifistic, matriarchal species. It makes you wonder about that other 1.6 percent, doesn't it? Looking at our closest relatives in nature, we could easily ask whether the aggression, selfishness, and competitiveness we see around us—and often believe is necessary for making it in the world—is alien to our physiology.

And although we've been programmed to celebrate these qualities with accolades like "Good for you: the highest grade in the class!" and rallying cries along the lines of "Get out on that field and knock 'em dead!" we tend to revere those whose strength has come packaged in gentleness. Far more people find role models in St. Francis and Harriet Tubman than in Alexander the Great and Genghis Khan.

Even so, women in particular can confuse being gentle with being a pushover, reverting back to a time when brute force ruled and lack of upper-body strength made one-half of the population subservient to the other. But gentleness—kindness, compassion, caring—does not detract from your power. On the contrary, it increases your power, and it just might help you get closer to a Higher Power that makes all things possible.

Can you envision how your life would be if you decided, fully and completely, to give up fighting? In this scenario, you wouldn't get to push your point for the pleasure of having someone else concede that you're right. You would help every co-worker as much as possible, even the one who might get your promotion if she starts looking too good. You would refuse to struggle with jeans that are too tight and a to-do list that is too full, and instead gracefully go with the larger size for now and put off till tomorrow what you really cannot do today. To live without fighting means calling a truce with your fellow humans, with yourself, and with life the way it is.

You may be thinking, "But what about child abuse and global warming and evil empires? We have to fight things like that or they'll *win*." There are certainly plausible arguments to support this position, but I wonder: How did everything get so confrontational? Where did we get the idea that it's all about fighting and winning or, the only other option, cowardice and loss? Mahatma Gandhi found that place in between: he called it *satyagraha*, "truth power." Martin Luther King Jr. resonated with the concept, added some ideas of his own, and the result was the nonviolent resistance that made equal rights regardless of race a legal mandate in America.

Centuries ago Buddha taught "kindness of action, speech, and thought"; Lao-tzu states in the Tao Te Ching: "I prize compassion; therefore I am able to be fearless"; and St. Paul advised, "Do not be overcome of evil, but overcome evil with good." These are not platitudes. They're the words of men who changed the world. (This was before women were allowed the change the world, but all the men who did it had mothers.)

The point is: Anybody can fight. Anger loves a good battle, and ego is pretty fond of it, too, as long as you're on top. It takes genuine courage and steely self-control to stand for the right without aggression or hatred. You do it, as Lincoln said, "with malice toward none, with charity for all." You do it by living with so much integrity that those around you want to follow suit. You do it by allowing circumstances to be as they are in this moment, and living in such a way that they'll be different in the next.

It won't work if you're selfish or faint-hearted. I learned this from a couple of fellows the night of my senior prom. I'll call them Josh and Randy because, in all honesty, I don't remember their names. No one had invited me to the big dance, but I said I wouldn't have gone anyway since I wanted to be part of an all-night peace vigil being held in a local park. (That was a lie, of course, contrived to save face and convince myself that I wasn't devastated about not having a boyfriend, not being "chosen.")

The protestors in the park thinned out as the night wore on until there were only half a dozen of us—Josh and Randy, three other women, and me—with blankets and sleeping bags, set to stay for the duration. Just after midnight a couple of men approached our little assembly, and I assumed they intended to join the vigil. When

169

the guys in our group arose to make space for them, the strangers started shouting insults and hurling punches.

Since I'd never seen a fight before, other than in the movies or on TV, I wasn't sure what to expect, but what I saw would have astonished even a habituated barroom brawler. Josh, a birthright Quaker with nonresistance in his bones, and Randy, a Vietnam vet who'd said, "I did my duty over there, and now I'm doing it here," stood stoically, arms at their sides. In about a minute, the attackers realized that no one was fighting back. They were so spooked by this lack of response that they hightailed it out of there as if they'd seen a ghost—two ghosts.

Randy was bleeding enough that one of the women took him to the ER, while Josh nursed his swelling jaw with a can of 7Up from the ice chest. I stayed awake to process in my mind what had happened. I didn't really know where I stood philosophically on questions like war and peace, or even personal self-defense. All these years later, I'm still not sure. In fact, compared with the myriad gray areas I see now, my world at seventeen was as black and white as a pair of spectator pumps. I don't know to this day if turning the other cheek is always the right response, but on that late spring night so long ago I was able to witness its power firsthand. That made up for missing the prom many times over.

I never crossed paths with Josh or Randy after that, but when the word *heroic* comes to mind, I see them and the images of heroes I've come to know since, some of whom are wearing military uniforms. All of them tapped into a strength they found within themselves to do what they believed was right. When you tap into your own gentle strength, you become a hero. Some people will admire you, some may think you've lost it, and most won't care either way. That's fine. When one drop of water is followed by another and another for a long enough time, boulders are worn away. You can choose to be like water. Or like a bonobo ape. Or like the person you hoped you'd become when you'd been on earth so briefly you could almost remember heaven.

Lucky Charm

What are you fighting right now? This might be a habit you want to break, a circumstance you want to change, or an injustice you want to eradicate. Whatever it is, get out of the ring for seven days. During this week, look for ways to bring about the change you seek without a fight.

171

Consider yourself lucky

Conduct yourself as if you were the luckiest person you know.

Any poker player will tell you: luck is a skill. You're not born with it; you make it. Once you understand that this is so, you can set about making some for yourself.

First, get a grasp on what luck is: being in the right place at the right time to intersect with fortuitous circumstances. How do you do this? Lots of ways. First, decide that where you are right now is a great place for said fortuitous circumstances to manifest. We waste a lot of potential luck presuming that it won't be ours until certain factors are in play—a better boyfriend maybe, or a bigger bank balance. Not so. Luck finds its way to penthouses and park benches. Put out the welcome mat.

Then, conduct yourself as if you were the luckiest person you know. I'm not telling you to start buying lottery tickets, but rather to go about your regular activities with the attitude that if there is luck in the vicinity, it will find you. When you hear yourself saying something like, "Just my luck," think, "Oh, yeah, my luck: I have so much of it."

Take all the luck that comes your way, and don't bypass any of it because it looks too small. A useful exercise is to pick up every coin you see. You won't get rich on small change, but seeing how much of it is in your path day after day can help open your awareness to the real riches (financial and otherwise) that can come to you.

My friend Mary Beth started picking up all the pennies and other coins she saw and saved them in a ceramic jar that the potter had labeled Seed Money. When the jar was full, she used the money to buy flower seeds that she planted in her garden. All season those flowers provided brilliant, blooming evidence of how riches can grow. Her attitude—and, she would tell you, her luck—changed markedly as a result.

Just as those flowers reminded Mary Beth of her good fortune, you can see everything around you and everything that happens to you as evidence of how lucky you are. Even the bag of discards you pack up to take to the charity drop box is a collection of valuables in someone else's eyes. See this and know this. And if you don't get the job or the part or the guy you were after, that's fine, too: you may have been spared something unfortunate, even though you thought it was what you wanted. Don't look back. Go forward knowing how lucky you are.

As you do this, it's perfectly acceptable to let others know that you see yourself as lucky. Unlike that poker player, you want to show your hand. One of my most inspiring friends often answers the innocuous question "How are you?" with, "Blessed and highly favored." I've heard her say this so many times that I can't help but see her the way she sees herself. There's nothing wrong with having everyone around you impressing on the universe that you are indeed a charmed human being, simply because you've trained them to see you that way.

And because you're one lucky duck, you have much to be grateful for. Bring this to mind over and over again. Mull over your blessings as you walk around town or go through your paces on the treadmill. See how many gifts and graces and lucky breaks you can think of while you're stopped at a red light. Count happy-making events in your life as you fall asleep at night. (There is a big, fancy word for "happy-making": *eudaemonic*. Nobody uses it outside spelling bees, but we can and start a trend.)

Being lucky is not a competition. Some people's luck may look more glamorous or more opulent, but you see only the part of their lives that shows. Things could be very different viewed from the inside out. Therefore, claim your own luck, be thankful for it, and pass it on via your example and your generosity.

175

Lucky Charm

Be grateful that you're a lucky person,
and go out and make some more luck.

41

Gather the gurus

The informal but venerable gurus
I'm alluding to are
our glorious girlfriends.

You are a great repository of wisdom. Some of it you brought with you when you showed up on earth. This is true for all of us. You can see it in children when they come out with those "kids say the darnedest things" statements. And you've gleaned additional wisdom during your lifetime. You've learned from education and experience, from mistakes and second takes, from heeding your intuition and from ignoring it and vowing not to do that again. Through practices such as meditation, keeping a journal, and jotting down your dreams when you awaken in the morning, you can access more and more of this inner knowing. Still, two heads are better. That's what gurus are for.

In addition to traditional gurus, spiritual teachers in the yogic tradition, there are guides and mentors and teachers of various sorts who enrich our lives. The informal but venerable gurus I'm alluding to are our glorious girlfriends. (Male friends are good, too, but most women seem to have only two or three guys who count as gurus and maybe six or ten or twenty other women.) Sometimes when I'm out with a few of my good friends, I find myself in awe of the amount of wisdom around the table. We might be talking about something as casual as makeup or movies, but I know that these sage and versatile women could converse just as easily about the meaning of life. Being with them is always a privilege.

This getting together comes naturally to us as women. Fascinating research from the University of Southern California determined that in addition to the well-known fight-or-flight response to stress, women (but not men) developed the additional response of "tend and befriend," gathering with children and other women for comfort, solace, and to figure out what to do next. It's mind-boggling to think that wanting to meet your best friend at Starbucks after an upset at work grew out of a modification in female brain chemistry that dates back to prehistory.

It isn't only in times of stress that we need to get together with our beautiful gurus, though. It's any time we want that comforting connection, an insight about something or other, or just to laugh and have fun and be reminded of our own magnificence. You gather your gurus whenever you get together formally or informally with the wise women in your world. Just going for lunch or coffee is good, and checking in by phone and e-mail keeps the connection current. You might also try one or more of the following:

Where the Wise Ones Are

Host a salon. Modern salons are a reinvention of the seventeenth-century salon movement in France in which the intelligentsia gathered in the homes of cultured women to further refine their sensibilities and discuss topics of the day. We can host salons to learn something (i.e., bring in a teacher or a speaker), address an issue in the community, or build a network of our gurus and other intriguing people of both genders.

A salon differs from a party in that casual conversation and food and drink are secondary to the raison d'être, the topic around which the gathering forms. A salon can be a onetime event or one of a series that allows for a wider variety of attendees. Newcomers bring with them new ideas and can prolong the life of a salon series.

Join or start a women's circle. This is a private group that meets on a regular basis (weekly, biweekly, or monthly) for a specific purpose—for example, spiritual growth, professional advancement, or support through an illness or shared concern. Some book clubs double as women's circles. Dottie Linscott founded one of these in Hansville, Washington. Because *Creating a Charmed Life* was the first book they studied, they christened themselves the Lucky Charms. (I borrowed their name for the action steps in this book.) Before the group disbanded after nearly nine years, they read scores of uplifting books and were inspired to such bold exploits as bringing me to Hansville. They booked the local community center for my talk and filled it to standing-room capacity.

When meeting privately as they usually do, women's circles range in size from five to fifteen members who share

179

in the decision making and determine the group's structure and activities. Some circles are informal discussion groups. Others include a ritual component such as having each participant light a candle at the start of the gathering and snuff it out at the end to delineate the "time apart" that the circle signifies. One element nearly all circles agree on is allowing each participant time to share without interruption, safe in the knowledge that there will be no feedback unless she asks for it. This is an assembly of equals, not group therapy.

The aim of a women's circle is to heal and foster growth in its members so they can in turn be agents of healing and growth in the world. In her book *The Millionth Circle,* Jean Shinoda Bolen writes: "What the world needs now is an infusion of the kind of wisdom women have and the form of the circle itself is an embodiment of that wisdom . . . a circle is nonhierarchical—this is what equality is like. This is how a culture behaves when it listens and learns from everyone in it."

Have a new-moon gathering. I was taken aback when, early in our friendship, Lane told me that she was part of a monthly new-moon group. Lane comes from an upper-crust Bermudan and British background. I expected her to be presiding over afternoon tea with some Lord and Lady, not cavorting outside to welcome the returning moon. She explained to me that this monthly gathering of women from all walks of life was simply a particular kind of women's circle, and that it was usually held indoors.

A coming together of women at the reemergence of the moon has historic precedence in many cultures. This point in the natural cycle is believed to be a powerful one, perfect for harnessing the energies of growth and renewal. Aware of this energetic boost, members of these groups often commit to embarking on some new undertaking or reaching a certain milestone before the next new moon.

Add a touch of class after class. Ask one guru-level friend (or several) to accompany you to a class, lecture, or bookstore reading. Afterward, go for dinner or dessert at a restaurant or someone's home and discuss what you heard. Sometimes you'll find that you get more from this after-the-fact review than from the event itself. At the very least, you'll receive insights you wouldn't have gotten on your own.

Connect with an action partner. An action partner is a co-guru of sorts: you and she check in by phone daily and share briefly with each other what actions you'll take to move your lives along. These actions can be in the realm of your work, relationships, self-care, or bringing a dream into reality—whatever is important to you. The next morning (or later in the day with a quick call or e-mail), you can share what you've accomplished. My action partner and I talk Monday through Friday at 6:30 a.m. She keeps me honest and focused and believing in myself, and I hope I do the same for her.

Partner for prayer. A prayer partner is someone with whom you make contact daily (by phone) or weekly (in person) for prayer. You can pray with each other and for each other. You can also recite affirmations, knowing that someone else has heard you speak the truth and that it's now your job to live it.

Grab a gratitude buddy. Your gratitude buddy is the person with whom you share what is at this moment filling your heart with gratitude. I think of it as counting your blessings in the presence of a witness. Simply making a gratitude list, keeping a gratitude journal, or reminding yourself of all you have to appreciate is a praiseworthy practice. Voicing it to someone else makes it all the more real.

Certainly professionals can fill some of our guru slots, and counselors, consultants, coaches, and others can be extremely helpful. Don't underestimate the value of your peers, however. The insight they give you has no price tag attached, but its value can be beyond measure.

182

Lucky Charm

Gather your gurus for lunch or tea.
Let them know that you see them
as teachers as well as friends,
and express your appreciation.

Prepare for your future

*If you want to feel good
about yourself later,
feel good about yourself now.*

I know sixty is the new forty and all that, but we still live in a society that celebrates youth and fears its opposite. If we're lucky enough to have a long life, we'll spend many years in midlife and old age. Of course you want to prepare for your future by taking care of your health and your money, but how about preparing on the inside? What kind of elder do you intend to be?

To a great extent, you are right now growing into the image you're holding. Is your older self someone who's vibrant and vital, content with the number of years she's spent on earth and living each day to the fullest? Or is the prospect of aging so frightening that you can't even hold an image of how you'll be? This is dangerous, because your mind, like nature, abhors a vacuum, and if you put nothing in there, images from a culture that does not appreciate older women nearly enough will step in to fill the space. Don't let them.

For your entire life to be charmed, start this minute to rethink your opinions of old age in general and your own in particular. Sociological studies repeatedly show that in countries and communities in which age is revered, the aged are healthier mentally and physically than in most of the Western world, where people worry about turning—heaven forbid!—thirty.

I've heard that there are Native American tribes in which both men and women are discouraged from offering an opinion on momentous matters until they reach seventy-five. Respect for the Elders Day (the third Monday in September) is a national holiday in Japan. Ayurvedic medicine, which developed in ancient India alongside yoga, offers the admonition: "Youth ends at sixty." This means that we have fifty-nine years to ensure health for later life, and also that after sixty we're no longer impeded by youthful distractions so our ideas can be trusted and our wisdom has weight.

If you didn't grow up with messages like these, old age can look like a desolate land, but it doesn't have to. Open yourself to the beauty that's there, first by finding the beauty in aged faces. We're so concerned with our laugh lines and our frown lines, and yet some of the most breathtaking faces on the planet belong to centenarians who lived in the sun and never used face cream. Appreciating this kind of beauty, the kind that is earned with time and experience, will help you appreciate your own loveliness throughout the life cycle. I'm not suggesting that you toss your sunblock and moisturizer. It's just that, no matter what you do, age has a way of showing itself, and we need to get over being fearful when it does.

Of course none of us can stem generations of conditioning that old is ugly and young is dazzling, but for self-protection we need to change our own outlook as best we can. Physiologically, birth to twenty-one is the maturation process, and twenty-one on is the aging process. That's a physical fact, and as such it has a place. Nobody ever based a charmed life on physical facts, however, and they define us only to the degree that we let them. Assert yourself in their presence by never devaluing yourself or anyone else because of age. Change your vocabulary: if *aging* sounds negative, call it *ripening*. If you find yourself thinking, "Ooh, he [or she] is looking so old," change that to "What an amazing talent he is!" or "What a great friend she's always been!"

And envision how you want your great-grandchildren to see you and know you. There are no guarantees in this life, but you can certainly hedge your bets. If you want to be healthy, take care of your health consistently, day after day, even when eating ice cream and watching TV sounds better than munching arugula and working out. If you plan to be mentally sharp, use your brain every day. Memorize poetry and phone numbers. Balance your checkbook without a calculator. Learn a language you didn't study in high school. Try to start and finish the *New York Times* crossword puzzle in one sitting. And finally, if you want to feel good about yourself *later,* feel good about yourself *now.* You are the right age, you have the right talents, and you even have the right limitations. I mean, if you didn't have limitations to work on, why would life keep you here long enough to become a great-grandmother?

French novelist and statesman André Malraux wrote with uncanny insight: "Youth is a religion from which one always ends up being converted." If you are devoutly young at this point, fabulous! It's a great time and a great ride. Don't miss an instant. If, on the other hand, you're approaching conversion, allow this to happen with style and finesse. It's easy to be a head-turning charmer at twenty-five. A woman who can do it at eighty blows everybody away—and not because she's on a first-name basis with her plastic surgeon. Start working on the attitude of agelessness. Trust me: it's not too early—or too late.

Lucky Charm

Spend a day with your grandmother—
or your grandchild.

Don't overlook the obvious

It's a new day only
when you approach
it in a new way.

Many of the techniques for having a life you love to live are obvious enough to miss. You might hear one of these and think, "Oh, yeah, I know that," but sometimes it's what we know best that we fail to do. To be sure you're not missing anything, I offer you:

10 Simple Charmers Too Helpful to Overlook

1. Start where you are with what you have. There are no prerequisites for stepping into your charmed life. You don't have to wait to begin the process until you've read more, learned more, or passed a test. In fact, the greatest obstacle is procrastination, the refusal to start where you are with what you have. All it takes is substituting one new, fresh attitude for an old, stale one, or implementing one new, life-affirming habit to displace one that is no longer doing you any good.

2. Focus on your vision every day. It's hard to reach a destination if you don't know where you're headed. That's why you need a vision of what your charmed life looks like. The vision can (and will) change as more and more of it becomes reality, but at any stage you don't want to leave an orphaned vision out there with nobody taking care of it. Take a little time, then, when you do your meditation or on your commute to work to think about the life you're creating. Even though you're *living* decidedly in the now, you can be *seeing* the expanded life of your vision and getting comfortable there. That way, when you've brought it into being, it will be fondly familiar.

188

3. Plan your day. Charmed lives are built a day at a time, so each one is significant. Therefore, map out your day at its beginning. Plan for the most efficient and productive working hours possible, and take equal care in apportioning the time that is fully yours. The steps called for today to bring your vision into being deserve a place on your calendar, so you'll give them the same attention you give everything else that's important.

4. If what you're doing isn't working, do something else. We waste a lot of time giving too many chances to a certain way of doing things. If that way doesn't work, scrap it and try something else. This also applies to what used to work just fine but no longer does. It's a new day only when you approach it in a new way.

5. Get enough sleep. After a sleep-deprived night, your day is destined to half measures. The amount of sleep you require is the amount you'd get if you woke up naturally, without a clock radio or alarm. For many people, that's *more* than the standard eight hours, yet a National Sleep Foundation poll found that a whopping 63 percent of us get by on less. The result is decreased productivity and creativity, and more impatience and crabbiness. (If this sounds like a description of your office, you're not alone.) In more extreme cases, lack of sleep makes people ravenously hungry while at the same time decreasing their glucose tolerance. It may even contribute to high blood pressure and heart disease.

In a charmed-life context, however, "get enough sleep" is far more than a miscellaneous health tip. Without sufficient shut-eye, you don't wake up raring to compose a gratitude list, meditate for twenty minutes, swim laps, and take on the world. Forces beyond your control—the baby cries, your spouse snores, the cat walks on your face at 4 a.m.— can interfere with a good night's sleep. This makes it all the more critical that you stay on top of everything that is in your control: get to bed on time; have a dark, soothing bedroom and a comfortable mattress; and scrupulously avoid caffeine after noon. If insomnia is a serious problem, consult a health practitioner. Your charmed life is at stake.

6. Actively implement the Golden Rule. Every culture has some version of "Do unto others as you would have others do unto you." It condenses into a sentence whole libraries of good advice on effective living. All decent people give its wisdom a nod. When, however, it becomes the basis for every dealing, relationships heal and charmed lives materialize where distressed ones were before. Use the Golden Rule from this minute on to guide your actions and even the thoughts you have about other people. Take it out of the "nice sentiment" category and make it intensely practical by putting into others' lives precisely what you want to show up, either as a first-time delight or a welcome encore, in yours. For example, if you're craving a massage, find a couple of tense folks and send their trapezius muscles to heaven. If you felt like a rock star when your recent houseguests marched into your kitchen and made you dinner, prepare a meal for someone who doesn't often get to enjoy that luxury.

190

7. Don't stop because it's hard. True, when something is "meant to be," there can be an inexplicable ease about it as roadblocks disappear and the necessary people and resources surface without a hitch. But a good percentage of the time, even what's supposed to happen needs some help to happen—help that usually entails quite a bit of hard work. We've all heard of the "overnight success" who has been at it for twenty years. As long as you believe that you're on the right path (and you can always check this out with people you trust and admire), don't stop just because it's difficult. You may need to change your approach or get additional assistance, but if what you want is worth going for, keep going.

8. Get a terrific haircut. It's only hair. It grows; it falls out. It may thin some as you get older, and we've all known and loved women whose bravery made us better people when they had no hair at all. Even so, since a good hair day is usually a good day in general, you may as well nudge the odds in your favor with a sensational haircut (or perm or wig or weave—whatever fits). You'll walk taller, feel prettier, and get compliments. "I love your hair" will never be on par with "I admire your character," but it's still nice to hear.

9. Adapt to a changing world. Life perhaps, and technology for certain, are changing today at a more rapid rate than ever before in history. It could be argued that the human nervous system was not designed to accommodate this degree of change, but we're here, it's now, and this is what we have to do. We can help ourselves by turning whatever resentment we might feel toward change into fascination. If we live long enough, we'll inhabit a series of different worlds during our tenure on earth. With a willingness to adapt, we can be right at home in each one of them.

10. Adjust when life has a different idea. It's important to have a plan and a backup plan. And if life has an idea that doesn't accommodate either one, we save ourselves a helping of grief by adjusting. This doesn't necessarily mean giving up on a dream, but it may call for some tweaking or rearranging, for a postponement or a detour. It may even turn out that the very change that seems to threaten your plan for yourself becomes the means by which that plan plays out. Whatever the twists and turns, the idea is to remain flexible and find balance when the parameters shift. It's rather like what a pilot does when he adjusts his altitude to bypass turbulence: it wasn't in the flight plan, but it's a welcome deviation.

In times that call for adjustment, you may find help, as I do, in seeing yourself as a spiritual entity, safe and protected in all circumstances. The affirmation I use most often during such periods comes from Paramahansa Yogananda: "At the center of peace I stand. Nothing can harm me here." If you can bring yourself to that center of peace (where you really already are), you can far more easily take life on its own terms without feeling that you've been betrayed or robbed of your self-determination. This is when you can see that life itself is your partner, and what you can cooperatively accomplish just might be beyond your wildest dreams.

Lucky Charm

The next time you're reminded
of a truism so obvious you're tempted
to overlook it, give it a little attention.
If it's something you can use,
find a place for it in your life.

44

Make something

Humans are supposed to make things.
It's why we have cleverness
and opposable thumbs.

You hear it sometimes: "The problem with this country is that nobody makes anything anymore." There's evidence for this assertion in the boarded-up factory and warehouse districts of many cities, and in towns abandoned by the single plant that had fueled their economy for generations. This manufacturing shortfall (to *manufacture* literally means "to make by hand") has trickled down from industry to individuals. We can *do* all sorts of things, but a great many of us fall short on being able to *make* anything useful or beautiful with our own hands. This may not affect the economy, but it affects our wholeness and sense of self. Humans are supposed to make things. It's why we have cleverness and opposable thumbs.

Besides, we're happy in the process of creating something real and solid. This is why physicians and psychologists suggest crafts such as knitting to their stress-laden patients, and why rehab programs for assorted ills all include the proverbial basket weaving or something similar. So, before somebody prescribes it and you can just enjoy it, make something. Make a hand-bound scrapbook or whole-grain dog biscuits, a crocheted muffler or a felt bookmark, a fresh-flower arrangement or a mini-collage greeting card—one the recipient will open, not download.

Be creative in your manual labor. My daughter, Adair, for instance, decided that she was paying too much for toiletries and started making her own. "Did you learn from a book?" I asked. "No," she said, "I just read the labels of the products I'd been buying and combined the ingredients I could understand and find." The results were eye cream (two tablespoons petroleum jelly, the oil from two coenzyme Q10 supplement capsules, and few drops of vitamin E oil); a facial masque (equal parts aloe vera gel and honey); and a customized scrub (one teaspoon each mild liquid soap and granulated sugar or, for sensitive skin, baking soda substituted for the C&H). The stuff works beautifully, and her off-the-grid grooming comes with a sense of pride as well as money saved.

Preparing food from scratch feels great, too. For some of us this could be as simple as making a salad that didn't come prewashed in a bag. Then there's my friend Elizabeth, who harvests mulberries from the big trees on her property and turns them into jam. She gathers watercress from a nearby stream for tea sandwiches. And lately she's been purchasing honey from local beekeepers and making mead, the time-honored wine once such a staple at weddings that the phrase "honey mead" has become the postnuptial *honeymoon*.

Endowed with neither artistic talent nor the self-sufficiency gene, I have found my attempts at making things to be less ingenious. I can't draw, but I am rather proud of a little sign I made, nicely mounted and framed, that instructs users of our bathroom in the feng shui prosperity practice of keeping the toilet lid closed when not in use. In the Lucinda Handwriting font and a lovely rose color, it states: "When the lid is down, the money stays around." Not much, I admit, but for someone artistically challenged, it is a tiny triumph.

If you know that you are capable of making something, do it. Otherwise, you could forget, and your children will never know that you could once hook rugs or can produce or carve toys out of wood. If you aren't able to make something now but you know you could learn how, do that. There are courses all over the place that prompt us to say, "This sounds interesting." It is interesting, *if* you sign up and get there.

195

Related to all this constructing is making sure that what's already here doesn't end up in a landfill before its time. In other words, if you can fix something (or get it fixed), do. It may be just as cheap to replace what's broken with a new edition, but there is a satisfaction factor, not to mention environmental brownie points, when you can give a second chance to some garment or object that still has life in it. Things are changing so rapidly anyway that giving some random possession a chance to last longer is a way to say to life: "Not so fast. I realize that the scene is changing before my eyes, but I'm getting my printer repaired and new soles for my gym shoes. These things at least will be with me for a while."

I have great respect for people who can make things and fix things. I love shoe-repair shops—the smell of the polishes, the accents of the cobblers, the new shoes that can materialize out of old ones time and again. It's also gratifying to buy the goods of artists and artisans, and know that you can own or wear something that is one of a kind and came into being from the play of human hands on a loom or sewing machine or potter's wheel.

There is a store in Greenwich Village in which up-and-coming jewelry artists and clothing designers rent booth space and offer their wares to the public. Among my finds from there is a simple skirt. It's black, nothing flashy or trendy. Its specialness is in the way it's cut—a swingy bias style you rarely see in ready-to-wear—and it gets positive attention every time I put it on. This gives me a chance to tell admirers that the skirt was designed by an artist I can visit and talk with, a person who can draw and could still cut and sew if she needed to. It's a real spirit lifter to learn that skills this authentic still exist—and that you don't have to be a millionaire to benefit from them.

Lucky Charm

Between now and next week,
either make something or learn how
to make something.

45

Enliven your diet

Fruits and veggies,
before they've been subjected
to heat or processing, are repositories
of life force that is transferred
to you when you eat them.

The essence of any charmed life is energy. This energy—the life force that the yogis call *prana* and that martial artists and traditional Chinese doctors call *chi*—inspires your best thinking and propels you toward your goals. Its magnetism attracts the best of life to come to you via other people and well-disposed coincidence.

During our lifetimes we operate with greater and lesser degrees of this life force. It's heightened when our stress levels are low, when we're taking good care of ourselves, and when we're happy. We increase our reserves by sleeping well and on a regular schedule; breathing deeply of clean, fresh air; and ingesting *prana* via the foods we eat. The foods that have the highest level of this subtle but vital energy are those that are *alive*.

Don't panic: I'm not suggesting that you join some insect-munching cult. By *living food,* I'm talking about fresh fruits and vegetables and juices made from them, and sprouts, nuts, and seeds—all of them uncooked, organic, and locally grown when possible. Fruits and veggies, before they've been subjected to heat or processing, are repositories of life force that is transferred to you when you eat them.

Some people eat these foods exclusively, and the "raw-fooders" I know appear to be in excellent health. I'm not suggesting that you take it that far, but if you can get to the point at which even 50 percent of the food you eat is in this category, your energy will soar, and you'll love how you look and feel.

Most nutritionists agree that raw produce is bursting with vitamins, minerals, and the phytochemicals believed to protect against degenerative disease. People who espouse the benefits of eating "high raw" sing the praises of enzymes, present in fresh foods but destroyed when subjected to cooking temperatures over 115 degrees Fahrenheit. They claim that we're born with an enzyme reserve but that we deplete it digesting cooked foods, which have no enzymes of their own. The theory is that raw foods—fruits, salads, freshly extracted juices—contain the enzymes needed for their own digestion and some to spare.

When making the transition to a high-raw diet, it is possible to experience detoxification symptoms, such as transient headaches and fatigue. (You can lessen these symptoms by using the suggestions in chapter 30, "Detox Your Body.") Three positive changes, however, are what most people notice almost immediately. First, if I may say this delicately, elimination improves. (Take my word here:

it *really* improves.) Next comes the heightened energy level. Within a few days, it's as if the weight of the world is off your shoulders and accomplishing what's in front of you seems easier than it used to. And finally, you look better. In addition to losing some weight (which will absolutely happen), it doesn't take long to get the fabled "raw-food glow" characterized by brighter eyes, clearer skin, and that infectious energy. When Adair was living at home, we used to do two weeks of raw food every summer. One of her friends asked why we did it, and she said, "Because everybody deserves to be gorgeous two weeks a year."

If you're intrigued, here's what you need to know to get started on the path to eating half (or more) of your food in the blissful state of alive and well.

Suggestions for an Enlivened Diet and a Livelier You

Start the day fresh. If you don't have a juicer, get one: the best first "meal" is fresh juice made of greens of your choice (I like romaine and kale), some apple or pineapple to make it tasty and sweet, and a little lemon and/or fresh ginger for some wake-up punch. Many people do beautifully on fresh juice first thing and fruit throughout the morning. If you want a heavier breakfast (or if you like your coffee), have that at least half an hour after your green juice.

Blend enlivening elixirs. Smoothies are a tasty, easy way to get more live foods into your diet. Use a base of water, fresh juice, or "nut milk"—a quarter cup raw hazelnuts or cashews blended with ten ounces of water and strained. Then add a banana (or two) and fresh or frozen berries. For a nutritional boost, make a "green smoothie" by tossing in some greens, such as romaine, spinach, or kale. They'll change the color but not the taste of your shake, and your body will be overjoyed to get them.

Create super-salads—and shoot for two a day. Many of us have been conditioned to think of salad as something on the side, or the item of choice when you don't want to be seen ordering the Philly cheesesteak. But a salad can be a delicious and hearty mélange of flavors and textures.

Choose a base of romaine, leaf lettuce, baby greens, spinach, arugula, or some combination, and add sprouts, tomatoes, carrot, radishes, cauliflower, cilantro—whatever looks yummy at the farmers' market. Give a salad soul-satisfying substance with crunchy sunflower or pumpkin seeds, chewy sun-dried tomatoes or cranberries, or spicy kimchi (Korean sauerkraut). Or opt for a cooked addition such as lightly steamed broccoli or steamed potato chunks, red beans, or garbanzos. (You can also blend salad ingredients with some water and appropriate seasonings—lemon pepper, basil, dill, a little sea salt—for soup. Avocado makes it creamy.)

Learn a few raw recipes. Although seasoned devotees usually eat simply, there is a whole world of live-food cuisine to tantalize the palate and give those who enjoy the culinary arts a new forum for their creativity. A properly wielded mandoline (thin slicer) or a sharp vegetable peeler can turn zucchini or a fat carrot into ribbons (like pasta) that are yummy with a marinara sauce made from ripe tomatoes, garlic, onion, and fresh basil. With a dehydrator, you can make crackers, crepes, pizza crust, and other ersatz wonders. For now, just learn to make a couple of simple salad dressings, soups, and desserts. You'll feel like a pro.

Bring on the reinforcements. Because we live in a cooked-food world, you may want to carry some raw food with you. Raw flax crackers (these can be made with a dehydrator or purchased at a health-food store) help when the bread basket is going around the table. A raw candy bar (some combination of dried fruit and nuts) in your bag means that when you meet a friend at the coffee place and she's enjoying a monster muffin, you can have a yummy treat, too.

Don't get cold. During the winter, make your salads from room-temperature ingredients instead of right out of the fridge, and leave the frozen fruit out of your smoothies. Heat your raw soups a little by using warm water in the recipe or gently heating the soup in a double boiler. (Use a kitchen thermometer to be sure you don't go over 115 degrees.) Even committed raw-fooders, if they tend to the cold side, often drink tea—antioxidant green tea, perhaps, or a tasty herbal such as licorice—when it's cold outside or somebody has cranked the AC up to high.

Go "live till 5." This little slogan helps many high-raw eaters stick with fresh raw foods during the day while leaving them free to enjoy a combination of raw and cooked foods for dinner.

As with any new undertaking, educate yourself. There are a plethora of books, DVDs, Web sites, and YouTube flicks offering information, recipes, and support. I recommend some of these in the "Resources for a Charmed Life" section at the end of this book. Take advantage of them. You deserve to be gorgeous and to have ample energy for a very charmed life.

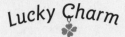

Lucky Charm

Eat at least one sizable salad
and three pieces of fresh fruit every day
from now on.

46

KC, here I come

It is a comfort to recognize
the dance of karma and consciousness.
In it lies the assurance that life
is not senseless and random.

KC is the abbreviation for Kansas City, my hometown, but here I'm using it to stand for something else: *karma* and *consciousness*. When you understand the respective roles of these two contributors to the state of your life, you're better able to accept what you can't fix and to more efficiently fix what you can. These are obviously huge areas of study, and yet they boil down nicely in the ditty "Life is half what you make it and half how you take it."

Your fifth-grade teacher probably explained Newton's third law as "Every action has an equal and opposite reaction," and if you went to Sunday school, you learned these words of Jesus: "Whatsoever ye sow, that shall ye also reap." These are ways of describing, in physical and spiritual terms, the principle that ancient Hindu sages called *karma*. Karma is cause and effect. Here's a simple example: Let's say you're a golfer intent on improving your skills. You sign up for lessons with a pro and go from playing nine holes to eighteen. You use your powers of visualization to see yourself making the shots, and you volunteer one afternoon a week to help young players with their putting. At the end the season, your scores have never been better. This is karma at work in a very pragmatic way. The lessons, the extra play, the mental focus, and sharing what you know are the cause; your superior game is the effect.

Obviously the workings of karma are not always this easy to follow. The concept grew from a tradition that accepts reincarnation, giving karma a very long reach and perhaps shedding some light on how bad things happen to good people and vice versa. Not a system of rewards and punishments, karma is rather the harvesting of seeds you've planted. If you plant turnip seeds, you can think "watermelon" with all your might, but you're going to harvest turnips.

Consciousness, on the other hand, is your perception of yourself and the world. Chris Michaels, author of *Your Soul's Assignment,* says, "Consciousness is the sum total of all your beliefs which create a mental atmosphere that surrounds you and attracts experiences—people, events, drama—into your life." Adjusting the angle of your awareness by bringing in a better belief can change your intuitional image of yourself the way putting on a nice, fresh outfit changes your image in the mirror.

The right consciousness can give you abiding joy in the present while creating a better future. Although it doesn't erase your karma, modifying your beliefs about yourself and your life makes the good times better and the bad ones easier to learn from and be done with. It can also make you more aware of the mysterious power of grace, which can turn up unexpectedly and carry you through anything.

In the rough-and-tumble of turns of events and states of affairs, it is a comfort to recognize the dance of karma and consciousness. In it lies the assurance that life is not senseless and random. Little children do not bring evil upon themselves, nor do terrible things happen because of the will of a capricious God. God is perfect, and so is your essential self. You have chosen to become incarnate in a plane of duality—*yin* and *yang.* It's as if we live on a bipolar planet that doesn't take its medication. Your soul knew that when you signed on to come here. It is only because you cannot have an overcoming without something to overcome that human life is equipped with resistance, the way a good gym is equipped with plenty of dumbbells and barbells and weight machines.

Despite what you may have heard, your level of material success does not necessarily correspond to the purity of your thinking or your closeness to your divine source. Of course you deserve a wonderful life, but spirituality should never be a kind of multi-level, sign-up-here, make-a-mint hucksterism. That insults every genuine spiritual teacher who's ever lived. The road to a life that is charmed in a mature and lasting way is that of realizing that we are not here to get everything our ego wants, and that pandering to selfish desires might lead to the fulfillment of those desires but not to profound joy or lasting peace. Try instead to first create lovely karma, and then, seek to expand your consciousness.

Create lovely karma. To do this, "Live up to the highest light you have and more light will be given to you." Peace Pilgrim said that. She was an amazing woman who spent the last half of the

205

twentieth century traversing America (and eventually other countries as well), almost entirely on foot, carrying the message that world peace will result only from inner peace. How close are you today to living up to your "highest light"? Is there something you're doing that doesn't jibe with that, or is there something you know you could be doing that has seemed too difficult or intimidating until now? Get closer to your inner light and your greatest aspirations through times of quiet reflection, and when you catch a glimmering of what living up to those would look like, act on it.

Expand your consciousness. This happens when you put yourself—thoughts, feelings, actions—on the highest wavelength you know of. Allow yourself ever greater expectations. Dream big, not just for yourself but for everyone. There is a Hindu prayer that says, "May all that have life be free of suffering." That's a big dream, the kind that can enlarge your consciousness. You won't do this perfectly. Just recommit daily and see how far you get. Einstein is said to have stated, "I want to know God's thoughts. The rest are details." It isn't just geniuses who can know God's thoughts. We all have a chance at it if we hang out where God does—the quiet place inside us, a lovely spot in nature that calms us, anyplace where we can infuse some beauty or lessen someone's pain.

By living up to your highest light and taking the high road with as many thoughts and actions as you can, you have a hand in both your karma and your consciousness. As a result, you'll find yourself worrying less, giving more, and getting a tremendous kick out of brightening whatever darkness you encounter every chance you get. Once you've been at it for a while, you'll notice that what you need to further your aims shows up more easily because your aims are in alignment with something bigger than your own desires. You'll meet the circumstances of your life—your karma, the good and the bad—with equanimity. And you'll use your consciousness to raise the collective consciousness. Is this a huge undertaking? You bet it is. Are you up for it? Without a doubt.

Lucky Charm

*Give some time today to taking a look
at your consciousness. This is big-picture stuff.
What do you believe about the world
and your place in it? What do you believe
is possible in your life? There is more to you
than you know. Whatever circumstances
you face today (your karma, if you will),
you can meet any of them and grow
from all of them.*

207

Proceed despite detractors

*Your assignment is to live a charmed life
in the midst of people
who don't believe you can do it,
and to accomplish this despite them,
not to spite them.*

Chances are there is at least one significant person in your life who thinks that all this charmed-life stuff is ridiculous. They may have told you to grow up, be realistic, and get with the program. Of course, it's *their* program, some variation on the theme of "Very few people do anything exceptional, and you won't be one of them." They might begrudge the time you spend reading books like this one and putting the suggestions you find there into practice. They may cite every time you've been sad or angry or things didn't work out the way you wanted as evidence that you're deluding yourself.

On the other hand, you could be living or working with people who are nice enough but who are convinced that they missed any chance at a charmed life a long time ago, and they don't think much of your odds either. They may never make a discouraging remark, but their sadness and resignation are like a black hole in the next cubicle or on the other side of the bed.

The task of charming a life becomes onerous in the face of criticism and even, if you're sensitive, in the presence of someone else's penetrating negativity. It's natural to want to respond by trying to explain yourself and prove your point, but that takes a pretty good talker. Negative people often lettered in debate. You may also be tempted to downplay your dreams and keep them to yourself. This works better than arguing, but too much censorship eats away at the soul. Your assignment, then, is to live a charmed life in the midst of people who don't believe you can do it, and to accomplish this *despite* them, not *to spite* them.

210

For starters, do a reality check and make sure that your actions and aspirations pass muster with your own rational mind and with the charmed-life peers and mentors who are helping you along. If they don't, you play right into the hands of the cynics—or even make a naysayer out of a potential supporter. For example, I know a woman who did one day's work as a movie extra. Some assistant director mentioned that she'd done well, and that was all it took to get her to give up her job—a good one that she'd liked a lot—to try to become an actress.

You have to know by now that I live on stories like "forty-two-year-old, never had a drama class, takes up acting." But even in my mind, "taking up acting" and "quitting the day job" are distinctly different animals. I was so shocked when she told me that I forgot to be encouraging and said instead, "You're kidding, right?" I hurt her feelings without intending to and didn't help at all.

Once you're certain in your own mind that the charmed life you're building is one that can exist in the world as we know it, you're ready for:

A Charmed-Life Guide to Coexistence

Let others be other. Extend to those around you the same respect and the same degree of autonomy you want for yourself, even if some of these people are not yet showing them to you. Allow your family, friends, and associates the dignity of their convictions, even if theirs are light-years apart from yours. You deserve the same consideration from them, of course. If you don't get it, rise above what they're unable to give and respect yourself even more.

Claim your autonomy. The fact that someone holds an opinion does not mean you have to share it. You can only live your own life, hold your own beliefs, and follow your own star. There's nothing that says you can't be a fine co-worker, friend, sibling, or mate, even when you and the other person choose to see something (or several things) differently.

As an autonomous being, you have every right to pursue your charmed life regardless of what anyone thinks about that. You may not want to advertise what you're doing by making your life list the screen saver on the family computer, but if some onlooker's opinion of what you're doing keeps you from doing it, you're playing into their hands and putting your autonomy out on the curb for pickup.

211

Refrain from trying to convert anybody. Some people turn the old saw "If you can't beat 'em, join 'em" into "If you can't beat 'em, get 'em to join you." It doesn't work. If you're expecting the best and detoxing your life, it might seem that the ticket to paradise would be to get your controlling spouse or your critical sister to try it, too. Nothing would be a bigger turnoff for them. Instead, don't say much (or don't say anything) about what you're doing. Just let it work in your life, and one day this person may come to you wanting to know how to get what you've got.

Take your doubts elsewhere. It's not always easy to remain positive, value yourself, honor others, and stay focused on the big picture. Sometimes you'll fall short, and you may wonder occasionally if it's even worth the trouble. This is when you need to turn to an action partner (see chapter 41, "Gather the Gurus") or another reassuring friend. It can be tempting to want to dump your doubts on anyone within earshot, but somebody who didn't understand what you were trying to do when it was working splendidly won't understand when it's going poorly, either.

Surround the person or people who don't understand with radiant light. When people are closed-minded, jealous, or just so sad that your happiness comes at them like a slap in the face, hold them in the light. Imagine them surrounded by it and soothed by it. See the light you're sending attaching to their own inner light. It may be down to a pilot, but it's in there, and the reinforcements you're sending will help it strengthen and grow.

If all else fails, get some distance. In most cases, you can create such good boundaries for yourself and live with such focus and self-containment that either the other person will make some changes or you'll be so content within yourself that it no longer matters if they change or not. Do everything within your power (and with the help of a Higher Power) to bring about this degree of contentment. If you've exhausted all avenues of advice and counsel, and you're working or living with someone who refuses to allow you to shine your own light, you may have to get some distance.

Relationships aren't always easy—"They're the advanced class," somebody told me—but getting a shot at a life on earth can't be a slam-dunk either. Living yours the way you want and striving to reach your highest potential aren't just little extras that are nice when you can get them. You've been entrusted with a precious life all your own. Although you owe those around you kindness, consideration, honesty, and respect, you owe yourself, and perhaps even your Creator, a life well lived.

213

Lucky Charm

*Just for today, tune out the doubters
and believe in yourself.*

Re-create a charmed life
if you have to

"The way we used to do it"
has to give way to
"Let's try something new."

Sometimes you have to do it over again.

It can happen like this. You've created a charmed life. It looks great from the outside and feels wonderful on the inside. All is well. Then everything falls apart (or maybe only one thing, but it's so enormous that it seems like everything). This is the test that separates the charmers from the charlatans. After the fire or the tornado, the death or the divorce, the pink slip or the dreaded diagnosis, just making it through is laudable. Making it through and coming out *better*—well, that's charmed-life country.

Nobody wants to start from scratch to redo what's already been done. It seems so tiring, so "been there, done that." And yet re-creating a charmed life is not an experiment in cloning. It's building anew, and it deserves the same excitement you'd give to building a summer home in Maine even though you'd already built a winter place in Florida. This second time around has to be its own challenge, its own adventure. You won't be making a photocopy of the way things used to be: you'll build on what you loved about your life then to create a life that is even more customized to the incredible human being you are today.

Obviously, this calls for flexibility. "The way we used to do it" has to give way to "Let's try something new." Otherwise you won't have a charmed life, just a below-par remake. The way things used to be was lovely indeed, the same way your kids were beautiful babies and now they're incredible people. You wouldn't want to confine them in infancy, and you don't want to confine the life you're meant to have now within the mold of one you had in the past, no matter how idyllic.

Janine is one reader who knows this well. For seventeen years, she lived luxuriously in Bermuda. She did it right, too, and made a point of being grateful for her beautiful home and her many opportunities to travel. She enjoyed her work, her husband, and her friends. Then one day with no warning, she got sick. Her condition was eventually labeled *chronic fatigue syndrome,* and on doctor's orders she and her husband sold everything and moved back to their native Jamaica, where neither had lived since their teens.

Confined to her room, she spent nearly a year looking out at the mountains and praying—holding the vision of good health and applying that aptitude for gratitude she'd developed previously to the blessings she knew would come. As she did this, her point of view shifted. The colors of the mountains were richer, the light at sunset more captivating. Her garden became a world of its own, blossoming as she did. The life Janine left behind no longer seemed as fulfilling as it once had, and she started to long for something else, something simpler—the very life she had now.

"I realize I'm living in a country with many social and economic problems," she says. "But I know now that each day is important to my soul. I know the charmed life can go on, despite setbacks, ill health, financial struggles, or country migration." I'd say that just about covers it.

Know this: If you ever made magic, you can make it now. If you once changed the circumstances of your life, you can change them a second time. If you were ever on top of the world, you can be there again, even if the world seems to be on top of you at the moment. You don't get just one shot at this, or a single golden opportunity that, once past, will never come again. Once you have the attitude and the tools for living a charmed life, you'll be able to craft another one if you have to. It won't be identical, but it will be ideal.

When you know that, you'll own your power. You'll feel safe. You'll find the bliss in every instant, the blessing in every breath. Despite some rerouting and reconfiguring and retracing your tracks at times, you can be assured that, moment to moment, you're living a life that works like a charm.

217

Lucky Charm

If you have to back up and patch up some aspect
of your charmed life, or should you ever need to
start again at the beginning, know that you have
the skills, the tools, and the grit to do it.

49

Love it.
Then maybe leave it.

Because love recycles and recirculates,
there is enough in you to give some
to this situation, even if you're looking
for a way to end it.

If a situation in your life ends before you come to love it, odds are you'll run into again. Oh, the names and faces will change, but circumstantially you'll be right back where you were five or ten or twenty years ago, again presented with the opportunity to learn to love.

This seems counterintuitive because we think of love as the "tie that binds." Indeed, that is its role in strong marriages, parent-child relationships, and when an artist loves a project or an activist loves a cause. But love is also necessary when ending a relationship or leaving a position, organization, or locale. This is because learning how to love is the primary purpose for being alive, and there is no way to make it an elective course.

Sometimes the lessons of love are easy to spot. Other times they're hidden in circumstances that aren't helping you blossom, that you really do need to leave or change. In cases like these, the last thing you're usually thinking of is how to *love* the noisy neighbors or the stifling job. It makes sense to think that if you came to love the situation, you'd attach yourself to it and never get out. Quite the contrary: until you love it, it's attached to you.

Oh, those neighbors may move, and you can go to work somewhere else, but you'll one day find yourself in eerily similar circumstances unless you allow love to perform its function as intangible Goo Gone. When you learn to love through any experience, that experience comes full circle, and you won't need to visit it again.

Two years after Patrick, my dear first husband, died, my daughter and I moved from Kansas City to the central Missouri Ozarks. The plan was to finish grieving, get my bearings, and figure out what to do next. I'd never lived in the country and didn't think I'd like it, but it was the best idea I had at the time. I made some wonderful friends there, and my little girl, then six, took to the outdoors and spent hours in imaginative play by our rocky stream. Still, I didn't really want to be there, so the idea of loving the place never crossed my mind.

When it was time to move on, the landlord from whom I'd rented for nineteen months refused to take my check for the final payment. He said that even though all my checks had been good before, I was moving away and if this one bounced, he'd have no way to get me ("with a hit man," I was thinking). While I was trying to figure out how to come up with cash on a Sunday in a town with no ATMs, the landlord took his electric screwdriver—I couldn't be making this up—and screwed the doors and windows shut, taking hostage my daughter, myself, and the half dozen friends who'd come to help us move. We had under ninety bucks as a group.

Then genius struck: Who had cash on a Sunday? The pastor! The collection plate, tithes and offerings: "Give and it shall be given unto you." I called the Disciples of Christ minister and told him that I desperately needed to cash a check for $267 and if he could help, maybe we wouldn't need to bring in hostage negotiators. He said he could do that, and an hour later my rent was paid in quarters and dimes and one-dollar bills. Upon our release, I said good-bye to our friends, put the three cats in two carriers in the backseat of the Toyota, and took off with my willing young companion for a new life.

But something wasn't right: there was unfinished business. That bit of drama with the landlord may well have been life telling me to come up with some love for the place I'd lived and appreciation for what it had taught me, or be "screwed" again in the future. But I didn't get the message.

Nearly two decades later, my current husband and I moved to upstate New York and I kept thinking, "This is so much like the Ozarks . . . Wow, they had one of these in the Ozarks . . . Why, I think I had to order propane in the Ozarks, too." Then I got it: I'd left my little rented cabin outside Camdenton, Missouri, without stopping to love the vast, placid Lake of the Ozarks and the breathtaking views of mountains so ancient they once dwarfed the Himalayas. I'd never thanked those woods and that stream for giving my daughter something I couldn't. And although I cared about my friends there, I hadn't loved nearly enough the way people I'd

221

known only a short time had taken a rudderless single mom and her offspring under their wing. They got us through a very hard time.

Now I was back—different zip code, different time zone, but the details were of little consequence. What was important was coming to love what this new place held for me. No one said I had to abandon my urban proclivities or stay in the country forever, only that it would be in my best interest to leave some love behind when I left. So I set to work.

What could I love? Well, I looked forward all weekend to the Monday-evening stretch class taught by an ageless gazelle of a woman who was once a Balanchine ballerina. And I was truly grateful for the natural-foods restaurant on the village green, the well-appointed fitness center at the edge of town, and the metaphysical bookstore with its sparkling lights and serene lecture hall. It was always a treat to stop in at the old-fashioned hardware store, the colorful produce market, and the Woodstock Farm Animal Sanctuary, where I could go any weekend to play with a three-legged goat or have my ear nuzzled by a steer whose enormity betrayed his gentleness.

As soon as I starting thinking about what I *could* love, I realized how much I *did* love. My life in Woodstock started to change at once. Our next-door neighbors who missed the city as much as I did moved back to Queens. A woman moved in who shared my interest in spirituality and world religions, and we knew immediately that we'd be soul-level friends. I started getting invitations to things and running into people I knew at the movie and the bakery. Even more profound, however, was that bringing some love to bear on my life as it was and where it was initiated a healing in me that, like all love-based healing, was retroactive. It could go all the way back to the day I was screwed into a little house at the Lake of the Ozarks and heal that, too.

So: What is present in your experience today that doesn't fit with what you think of as a charmed life? What can you find in this place or person or post or dilemma that you're able to love? Is it the irony that you graduated from Cornell magna cum laude and now you're working a temp job that could be done by a German shepherd with adequate training? Or, if you had a marriage or love affair that went pickle-barrel sour, can you love the person for the qualities you once saw, the sweet times you had, the lessons you learned?

Because love recycles and recirculates, there is enough in you to give some to this situation, even if you're looking for a way to end it or you're already out the door. If you can't seem to find this love in yourself, ask God for some extra and expect an answer to your prayer. When you have it, you can end a relationship without ill will. You can leave a job with the loose ends tied up so the next person can love it from her first day. And you'll walk away free and clear, today and forever.

223

Lucky Charm

Start the process today
of loving something in your life
that you didn't think you would.

50

Be the one to prove this stuff

When you see more fun and more depth
coming arm in arm into your life,
you'll know you're on target.

Because you picked up this book and have read it to the end, I believe I'm safe in assuming that you are an *extra-dimension person*. That is, you believe that life is not a series of random events to get through, collecting trophies as you go; rather, you believe that you are here *on* purpose and that you came here *with* a purpose. You're interested in empowerment for yourself and others. You sympathize with the victims, but you're in league with the overcomers. You know that hope is always a valid state of mind and that there are forces in play that help us along. And although I can't know this for sure, I suspect you believe that life is a continuum and that this time on earth is but one facet of our total experience.

Whatever the specifics of your worldview, it's up to you to live it. It doesn't matter who *says* you can change your life. It's only a hypothesis until your life changes. Everyone knows that espousing a belief is far easier than living it. This goes for people who read books like this one and those who write them. Part of human nature is to be enthusiastic when things are going well and lose steam when they aren't. We've all been there: "Saying these affirmations every morning is incredible! I'm getting along so well with my boss and I've stopped eating sugar and don't even miss it!"

But then the boss has a meltdown and somebody brings in birthday cake, and the erstwhile status quo reinstates itself as if you'd never affirmed a thing. But you did. Your work—whether affirmations or prayer or going to a therapist and learning how to stand up for yourself—changed you deep inside. You can go back to work knowing that you and your supervisor now have a history of getting along, and you have a history of making it from breakfast to lunch and lunch to dinner without cake. In other words, there will be setbacks. Just don't let them set you back any more than necessary.

In order for you to live a charmed life a day at a time, as well as look back with some hindsight and see how far you've come, you have to maintain both your belief and your focus, whether you're coasting effortlessly or trudging uphill. It's going to take some self-discipline to do what you need to do every day to net a remarkable life. If that weren't the case, more people would be doing it.

Obtain the support you require, and keep yourself inspired to the hilt. Get steady input from books, audios, informative lectures, and uplifting films, as well as from the people you know who are also committed to charmed living for themselves and for you.

You can't expect to get much of this support and inspiration from the world at large, because a great many men and women have boxed themselves so tightly into a single way of seeing things that they're threatened by anything beyond that. Similarly, the mass culture, for the most part, is not invested in your having a charmed life. It's much too creative a stance to take. You could make waves, or stand for something and not back down. You might approve of yourself so much that you wouldn't need to buy everything the advertisers want to sell you to reach some impossible standard of "good enough."

Your charge, if you're game, is to create your own charmed culture within society as it exists right now. Of course you're part of the world like everybody else. You stay abreast of things and know what's going on, while at the same time constructing a foundation for your dreams regardless of what is going on.

This is your chance: You're on center stage, and you've just heard your cue. This is your opportunity to be the one to prove what you stand for. Of course it would be nice to prove it to everybody else, to get your significant other meditating with you and your mother thinking so positively you would swear she was channeling Norman Vincent Peale. But the person you really have to convince is you. When you see your life operating on a higher level because you're working with the Law of Expectation, keeping a serendipity log, and staying close to what makes you come alive, you'll want to keep it up and learn more. When you see more fun and more depth coming arm in arm into your life, you'll know you're on target.

Once you realize that you really *are* living a charmed life, the ideas and actions you've garnered from this book and elsewhere will no longer be tentative and theoretical. You'll have proven them for yourself in the laboratory of your home and office, in traffic and on the subway, when you're tired and your feet hurt and someone says the kind of thing that used to make you feel small. You'll find yourself suspecting that, regardless of what is taking place around you, everything you need is within you. When you know that for certain, the rest is mere accessorizing.

Lucky Charm

See yourself as a scientist today. You're not one to simply read and learn the theories. You're going to test out those that strike a chord with you and prove them in your own charmed life.

228

Resources for a Charmed Life
(by chapter)

Introduction

The predecessor to this book is *Creating a Charmed Life: Sensible, Spiritual Secrets Every Busy Woman Should Know* (San Francisco: HarperSanFrancisco, 1999). It contains seventy-five tiny, prescriptive essays on topics ranging from "Play Your Free Square" (like the free square on the bingo card, there's one in your life) to "Practice the Vacation Principle" (and live like you're on vacation every day).

Chapter 1, "Know that you are worthy"

I Am Grateful: Recipes and Lifestyle of Cafe Gratitude, by Terces Engelhart (Berkeley: North Atlantic Books, 2007), is a beautiful, kitchen-friendly guide from the cofounder of the restaurant where I had the worthiness epiphany. The emphasis is raw food, even though the "I am worthy" dish I ordered was cooked. And if you'll be in California, there are Cafe Gratitude locations in San Rafael, San Francisco, Berkeley, and Los Angeles.

Chapter 5, "Wake up and smell the morning"

The book with the clock as its frontispiece and the instruction to get up an hour earlier than usual for exercise, meditation, and spiritual study is *Invitation to a Great Experiment: Exploring the Possibility That God Can*

Be Known, by Thomas Powers (New York: Crossroad, 1990). It is out of print but available used and in libraries. I love this book. People have had study groups based on it that have gone on for years; there's that much to delve into.

Chapter 6, "Expect the best"

There are to my knowledge no books on the Law of Expectation, but on the related (and more popular) topic of the Law of Attraction, quite a bit has been written. I like *The Law of Attraction: An Introduction to the Teachings of Abraham,* by Esther and Jerry Hicks (Carlsbad, CA: Hay House, 2006).

Chapter 7, "Give something away today"

I am indebted for this practice to the superb prosperity coach and seminar leader Paula Langguth Ryan. Her books include *Giving Thanks: The Art of Tithing,* with a foreword by the Reverend Catherine Ponder (Odenton, MD: Pellingham Casper Communications, 2005). Paula's Web site is www.artofabundance.com.

Chapter 10, "Make life-charming decisions"

The song "Grateful," by John Bucchino, can be found on the CD *Grateful—The Songs of John Bucchino.* Michael Feinstein sings the title cut, and although you can certainly download this song from iTunes, the entire CD is a treat, featuring legendary singers including Judy Collins, Liza Minnelli, Patti LuPone, and Kristin Chenoweth. Find it in stores or on the composer's Web site, www.johnbucchino.com.

Chapter 12, "Wash the dishes with all your heart"

The act of giving yourself fully to the activity at hand is what the Buddhists call *mindfulness.* Jack Kornfield, a Buddhist teacher, draws on his own tradition as well as Christian, Jewish, Hindu, and Sufi teachings in his heartwarming book *After the Ecstasy, the Laundry: How the Heart Grows Wise on the Spiritual Path* (New York: Bantam Books, 2001).

Chapter 13, *"Dress for the occasion"*

I really like to read books about clothes. I think it takes me back to the "charm school" classes I took at Montgomery Ward every autumn of my early adolescence. A favorite of these books is *Before You Put That On: 365 Daily Style Tips for Her,* by *Today Show* contributor Lloyd Boston (New York: Atria Books, 2005).

You also can't go wrong with anything from image consultant Brenda Kinsel—I read everything she writes. Her latest is *Brenda Kinsel's Fashion Makeover: 30 Days to Diva Style* (San Francisco: Chronicle Books, 2007).

Oh, and speaking of an Audrey Hepburn style manual, one I like a lot is the adorable little guide *What Would Audrey Do?* by Pamela Keogh (New York: Gotham Books, 2008).

Chapter 14, *"Slow down"*

I've read a lot about getting more hours into a day, but I always return to *Slowing Down to the Speed of Life: How to Create a More Peaceful, Simpler Life from the Inside Out,* by Joseph Bailey and my friend the late Dr. Richard Carlson (San Francisco: HarperSanFrancisco, 1998).

Chapter 16, *"Become surprisingly fit"*

I'm focusing on classics here, but the fitness books that convinced me to commit to exercise are tried and true. For cardio conditioning: *The New Fit or Fat,* by Covert Bailey (New York: Houghton Mifflin, 1990). For strength training: everything in Miriam Nelson's "strong women" series, notably *Strong Women, Strong Bones,* cowritten with Sarah Wernick (New York: Perigee Trade, 2006), and *Strong Women Stay Young* (New York: Bantam Books, 2005). And for flexibility (in every sense of the word), the yoga book I refer to most is the amply illustrated *Yoga Mind & Body,* by the Sivananda Yoga Vedanta Center (New York: DK Publishing, 1998).

Chapter 18, "Live richly"

Charles Fillmore, who's quoted as having said, "Poverty is a sin," was the cofounder of the Unity movement. You may know Unity from its little devotional magazine, *Daily Word* (www.dailyword.com). Among Fillmore's many books is *Prosperity: Discover the Spiritual Secrets to a Life of Abundance and Purpose* (New York: Jeremy P. Tarcher / Penguin, 2008).

The Web site for Debtors Anonymous, mentioned in this chapter, is www.debtorsanonymous.org. A book that explains the DA program and has turned around many, many financial lives is *How to Get Out of Debt, Stay Out of Debt, and Live Prosperously,* by Jerrold Mundis (New York: Bantam Books, rev. 2003). His Web site is www.mundismoney.com.

Barbara Stanny's *Prince Charming Isn't Coming: How Women Get Smart About Money* (New York: Penguin, rev. 2007) is a real eye-opener from a woman whose inheritance was squandered by her gambling-addicted ex-husband. She got smart and is now a top author, speaker, and coach with the mission of inspiring women to become financially empowered. Her Web site is www.barbarastanny.com.

Another personal-finance book I highly recommend is *It's Not About the Money: Unlock Your Money Type to Achieve Spiritual and Financial Abundance,* by Brent Kessel (San Francisco: HarperOne, 2008). Kessel is a high-level financial adviser whose practice of yoga and meditation led him to successfully combine spirituality and wealth management. His Web site is www.brentkessel.com.

Chapter 20, ". . . Then connect with the rest of us"

Whether you're a natural networker or quiet and shy, there's a great deal to learn and enjoy in Leil Lowndes's *How to Talk with Anyone: 92 Little Tricks for Big Success in Relationships* (New York: McGraw-Hill, 2003). This book will teach you the fine points of making a first impression, mastering small talk, and making your phone a powerful communications tool. The author's Web site is www.lowndes.com, and if you get on her e-mail list she'll send you the occasional stunning tip for conversational brilliance and becoming a people magnet. (She wrote a book about that, too.)

Chapter 21, ". . . And sometimes savor solitude"

Alice Marie Bergman, the woman who took herself on a private retreat and bought those *Sex and the City* stilettos, is a wonderful singer, songwriter, podcaster, and mom—someone you might want to know. Her Web site is www.teawithalicemarie.com.

And *the* comprehensive guide to retreats of every sort is Jennifer Louden's *The Woman's Retreat Book: A Guide to Restoring, Rediscovering, and Reawakening Your True Self—In a Moment, an Hour, or a Weekend* (San Francisco: HarperSanFrancisco, 2005).

Chapter 22, "Add a splash of red"

How about a red book? *The Red Book: A Deliciously Unorthodox Approach to Igniting Your Divine Spark* (San Francisco: Jossey-Bass, 2006) is written by the totally engaging Sera Beak (I've met her and she's a peach), a Harvard-trained scholar of mysticism and comparative religions. She is intent on spearheading what she calls a "Redvolution" of awakened spirituality, focusing in particular on women in their teens, twenties, and thirties. Her Web site is www.serabeak.com.

Chapter 23, "Grow green gracefully"

Watkins Books in London, the shop where I first learned the word *ecology,* is still a fixture in Cecil Court, a charming lane near Trafalgar Square replete with specialty booksellers. The Web site is www.watkins-books.com.

Scores of books have come out in recent decades about living in a way that cares for the earth, but some were dreary and righteous. It's a new day in the green-guides department! The one I quoted (and find myself referring to time and again) is *Gorgeously Green: 8 Simple Steps to an Earth-Friendly Life,* by Sophie Uliano, with a foreword by—no kidding—Julia Roberts (New York: Collins, 2008). Uliano covers environmentally sound living—home, fitness, beauty, style, food, travel, gardening—with panache, and she gives lots of specific product and Web site recommendations. Her own site: www.gorgeouslygreen.com.

Another unusual take on the topic is *Go Green, Live Rich: 50 Simple Ways to Save the Earth (and Get Rich Trying),* by David Bach with Hillary Rosner (New York: Broadway Books, 2008). In it financial guru Bach (his Web site is www.finishrich.com) counters the contention that an eco-lifestyle has to be expensive. With chapters such as "Unplug It" and "Bring Your Lunch to Work," he shows readers how going green can actually save them money.

Also, for anyone who read here for the first time about the connection between animal agriculture and greenhouse gases, here is a quotation from the United Nations Food and Agriculture Organization (FAO) Newsroom (www.fao.org), citing a 2006 report: "According to a new report published by the United Nations Food and Agriculture Organization, the livestock sector generates more greenhouse gas emissions as measured in CO_2 equivalent—18 percent—than transport. It is also a major source of land and water degradation."

If this piques your interest in exploring a plant-based diet, a terrific (and delicious) guide for the skeptical is *How to Eat Like a Vegetarian Even If You Never Want to Be One,* by Patti Breitman and Carol J. Adams (New York: Lantern Books, 2008).

Chapter 24, "Keep your sunny side up"

There are dozens, possibly hundreds, of worthy books about positive living, but the great-granddaddy of them all is *The Power of Positive Thinking,* by Norman Vincent Peale (New York: Fireside / Simon & Schuster, 2003). Although some of the language is understandably dated (this book was first published in 1952), the longtime pastor of New York City's Marble Collegiate Church presents information that is as fresh as this morning and useful right now.

Chapter 27, "Put fear in its place"

A soothing and useful guide for facing fear and turning it into joy is *The Places That Scare You: A Guide to Fearlessness in Difficult Times,* by Pema Chödrön (Boston: Shambhala, 2002). Chödrön is an American Buddhist nun in the Tibetan tradition, and she has found a way to apply time-honored techniques to quelling the fears that plague us today.

I also mention in this essay that caffeine consumption can exacerbate fear and anxiety in susceptible people. If you think you might be one of them, I recommend *Caffeine Blues: Wake Up to the Hidden Dangers of America's #1 Drug,* by researcher and clinical nutritionist Stephen Cherniske (New York: Warner Books, 1998).

Chapter 29, "Write yourself a life list"

When the good people at Martha Stewart's *Body+Soul* magazine asked me to write a story about life lists (that article, "What's on Your Life List?" appeared in the April 2008 issue of *Body+Soul*), they introduced me to Michael Ogden, coauthor with Chris Day of the definitive book on the topic: *2Do Before I Die: The Do-It-Yourself Guide to the Rest of Your Life* (New York: Little, Brown, 2005). The book details the process of making a life list and is filled with stories of people who fulfilled a wide variety of life-list intentions, from honeymooning in the Galápagos to walking on hot coals to finding a birth mother. Ogden and Day's Web site, www.2dobeforeidie.typepad.com, lets you see other people's lists (with some ten thousand intriguing I wannas) and post your own.

Quoted in chapter 29 is Barbara Biziou, a life coach and specialist on the importance of ritual for contemporary men and women. She is the author of *The Joy of Ritual: Recipes to Celebrate Milestones, Transitions, and Everyday Events in Our Lives* (New York: Golden Books, 1999). Her Web site is www.joyofritual.com.

I also mention in this chapter Napoleon Hill's *Think and Grow Rich,* among the first and still one of the best books in the control-your-destiny genre. A new edition, revised and updated by Arthur Pell, with contemporary success stories woven in, is *Think and Grow Rich: The Landmark Bestseller—Now Revised and Updated for the 21st Century* (New York: Jeremy P. Tarcher / Penguin, 2005).

Chapter 30, "Detox your body"

A helpful book to start with on this topic is *Health Bliss: 50 Revitalizing NatureFoods and Lifestyle Choices to Promote Vibrant Health,* by Susan

Smith Jones, with a foreword by Louise Hay (Carlsbad, CA: Hay House, 2008). Susan has been at this for many years. She overcame a crippling accident and went on to become an athlete and health guru.

Another terrific book on detoxing and starting fresh by taking small, nonthreatening steps is Kathy Freston's bestselling *Quantum Wellness: A Practical and Spiritual Guide to Health and Happiness* (New York: Weinstein Books, 2008). Freston also emphasizes the importance of caring for others as we progress toward self-healing.

To find out more about Bikram yoga, the first and "official" yoga done in a hot room, visit www.bikramyoga.com.

There are also a couple of products mentioned in this chapter that might be new to you. One is *kombucha,* a fermented tea that was called the "immortal health elixir" in ancient China. Enthusiastic home brewers make their own from culture, but I find it bottled and ready to drink in the refrigerator section at the health-food store; the brand name is GT's Organic Raw Kombucha (www.gtskombucha.com). The other product of interest is Teeccino (www.teeccino.com), a caffeine-free herbal "coffee." It's roasted like coffee, and you brew it using a coffeemaker, espresso machine, or French press, giving it a delicious aroma and the richness of the real thing. 237

Chapter 31, *"Detox your life"*

In the area of life detox that has to do with establishing order, if you're in the market for a top-notch organizing pro, check out www.napo.net, the site of the National Association of Professional Organizers.

An organizing book that has been a godsend for me—probably because it doesn't seem like an organizing book—is *Scaling Down,* by Judi Culbertson and Marj Decker (Emmaus, PA: Rodale, 2005). Its subtitle is *Living Large in a Smaller Space,* and it's geared to people who are downsizing. (I received it as a gift when my husband and I moved to the country, becoming possibly the only people in history to move out of Manhattan into even less square footage.) But I think *Scaling Down* would help anyone get organized, even if he lived in a loft or a mansion.

Another helpful read for clearing space and keeping it that way is *Clear Your Clutter with Feng Shui,* by Karen Kingston (New York: Broadway Books, 1999). Kingston bypasses the more esoteric and, to the Western mind, inexplicable aspects of feng shui and brings the ancient art to bear on today's crowded closets and overburdened desks. I read it at least once a year just to stay on top of things. In the same genre but focused on a more subtle level is *Space Clearing A–Z: How to Use Feng Shui to Purify and Bless Your Home,* by Denise Linn (Carlsbad, CA: Hay House, 2001), a dandy spiral-bound guide to getting the energies in your home to sparkle.

Laurie Sue Brockway, who contributed the suggestion for dancing as a space-clearing ritual, is an interfaith minister, wedding specialist, and the author of enchanting books including *A Goddess Is a Girl's Best Friend* (New York: Perigee Trade, 2002) and *The Goddess Pages: A Divine Guide to Finding Love and Happiness* (Woodbury, MN: Llewellyn Books, 2008).

Chapter 32, "Fill your life with beauty"

When it comes to living beautifully, the work of Alexandra Stoddard is superb. She is an interior designer and prolific author with many recent and wonderful books, but the gold standard in the "surround yourself with beauty" category is her timeless *Living a Beautiful Life: 500 Ways to Add Beauty and Joy to Every Day of Your Life* (New York: HarperCollins, 1988).

Letting the Lotus Bloom: The Expression of Soul Through Flowers, quoted in this chapter, is part memoir and part love story between floral designer Kevin Joel Kelly and the flowers with which he has worked for twenty-five years (Kansas City, MO: Llumina Press, 2006, with a foreword by Thomas Moore).

Chapter 33, "Do the cosmic two-step"

The books in connection with which I appeared on *The Oprah Winfrey Show* are my *Shelter for the Spirit: Create Your Own Haven in a Hectic World* (New York: HarperCollins, 1998) and *Lit from Within: A Simple Guide to the Art of Inner Beauty* (San Francisco: HarperSanFrancisco, 2002). *Shelter for the Spirit* grew out of my years as a single mom trying to create a "real home" for my daughter and me. Once I felt that I'd succeeded, I wrote the book to explore how, through such simple activities as cooking, cleaning, simplifying, and celebrating, anyone under any circumstances can make a home that nurtures the soul. *Lit from Within* explores inner beauty—how it's not just the consolation prize for a lack of the outer kind, but rather the root from which all beauty arises.

I mention in this chapter the term "vision board." A vision board or "treasure map" is a visual rendering of the life you want, usually a collage of words and pictures clipped from magazines and glued to poster board. A chapter in *Lit from Within*, "Map Your Dreams," details the process.

Chapter 34, "Indulge in your simplest pleasure"

You'll need to come up with your own simplest pleasure, of course, but if you share mine—soaking in a hot tub—you may enjoy a fine treatise on the subject, *The Art of the Bath,* by Susannah Marriott (London: MQ Publications, 2004), covering various sorts of baths and the enticing accoutrements of each one.

Chapter 35, "Take train trips and road trips"

For a peek at train travel at its finest (e.g., via the Orient Express and the California Zephyr), delve into *First Class: Legendary Train Journeys*

Around the World, by Patrick Poivre d'Arvor (New York: Vendome Press, 2007). It even comes with a slipcase box that looks like a steamer trunk!

For practical train-travel info, an excellent guide is the sixth edition of *USA by Rail,* by John Pitt (Chalfond St. Peter, UK: Bradt Travel Guides, 2005). It shows you where you can go by train (both U.S. and Canadian destinations), complete with schedules and a listing of railway museums.

Or simply hop onto www.amtrak.com.

Leonard Peters's *Love and Awakening in America,* about his cross-country car trip, is as of this writing still in process. Therefore, I cannot provide publication information, but it promises to be a vicarious adventure.

Chapter 36, "Claim a cafe"

Few writers write for their fellow writers with the beauty and insight of Natalie Goldberg. Her books that have inspired me (and taught me to write in coffee shops) include *Wild Mind: Living the Writer's Life* (New York: Bantam Books, 1990), *Writing Down the Bones: Freeing the Writer Within* (Boston: Shambhala, expanded ed., 2005), and *Thunder and Lightning: Cracking Open the Writer's Craft* (New York: Bantam Books, 2000).

Chapter 37, "Be completely, utterly yourself"

The book that reminded me of the exquisite promise of the ten-year-old girl, and what too often happens to that promise as the girl makes her way to womanhood, is *Reviving Ophelia: Saving the Selves of Adolescent Girls,* by Mary Pipher and Ruth Ross (New York: Riverhead Trade, 2005). I read it (in an earlier edition) to help my daughter through her adolescence and found that it did as much, if not more, to help me heal wounds left over from mine.

Camille Maurine, who made that grand entrance to the London restaurant, is the coauthor with her husband, Lorin Roche, of *Meditation Secrets for Women: Discovering Your Passion, Pleasure, and Inner Peace* (San Francisco: HarperSanFrancisco, 2001). This is an inviting, feminine look at the practice of meditation with twelve themed chapters focusing on such topics as claiming your inner authority and loving your body.

Chapter 39, "Give peace a chance"

Being Peace, by Thich Nhat Hanh (Berkeley: Parallax Press, 2005), explores simple but powerful practices for finding peace in oneself and bringing peace to the world.

The Essential Gandhi: An Anthology of His Writings on His Life, Work, and Ideas, edited by Louis Fischer, with a preface by Eknath Easwaran (New York: Vintage Spiritual Classics / Random House, 2002), distills the work of this man whose life for many embodies the essence of gentle strength.

Kate Lawrence offers a fascinating guide for contemporary peacemakers in *The Practical Peacemaker: How Simple Living Makes Peace Possible* (New York: Lantern Books, 2009). In her short but powerful book, Lawrence shows how, through simple changes in diet, shopping practices, media habits, attitude, and lifestyle, we can be active promoters of world peace as we go about our daily lives.

Chapter 41, "Gather the gurus"

The Millionth Circle: How to Change Ourselves and the World—The Essential Guide to Women's Circles, by Jean Shinoda Bolen (Newburyport, MA:

Conari Press, 1999), is a manual for creating women's circles and a testament to the belief of the author, a Jungian psychologist and bestselling author of *Goddesses in Every Woman*, that enough of these circles just might change the world.

Naomi Call, a life coach and the author of *Yoga in Bed: Awaken Body, Mind, and Spirit in 15 Minutes* (Findhorn, Scotland: Findhorn Press, 2005), has information on her Web site about women's gatherings, particularly new-moon groups. Check this out at www.naomicall.com.

Chapter 43, "Don't overlook the obvious"

That quotation from Paramahansa Yogananda, "At the center of peace I stand. Nothing can harm me here," comes from his *Metaphysical Meditations* (Whitefish, MT: Kessinger Publishing, 2007).

242

Chapter 44, "Make something"

A comprehensive guide for concocting your own toiletries as my daughter does is *Organic Body Care: Homemade Herbal Formulas for Glowing Skin and a Vibrant Self,* by Stephanie Tourles (North Adams, MA: Storey Publishing, 2007).

The shop where I found that wonderful skirt is EdgenyNoho (online at www.edgeny.com), and the gifted designer—you heard it here—is Johanna Martinez.

Chapter 45, "Enliven your diet"

The raw-food recipe book I use most often is *Raw Food Made Easy for 1 or 2 People,* by Jennifer Cornbleet (Summertown, TN: Book Publishing Company, 2005). It uses recognizable ingredients found in any supermarket or health-food store and requires no equipment other than the blender and food processor you already have. From soups and dips to puddings and pies, the results are scrumptious and the preparation a breeze. Jennifer's Web site is www.learnrawfood.com; there you can find the book's companion DVD.

Another useful volume for anyone interested in living foods is *The Raw Revolution Diet: Feast, Lose Weight, Gain Energy, Feel Younger,* by Cherie Soria, Brenda Davis, and Vesanto Melina (Summertown, TN: Book Publishing Company, 2008). While many books on this subject are intuitive and anecdotal, espousing the glory of raw based on personal experience, chef Soria (founder of the Living Light Culinary Arts Institute in Fort Bragg, California) saw the need for a book that provides not only how-to info and delicious recipes, but also unassailable nutritional backup. Therefore, she brought on as coauthors two registered dieticians who were not raw-fooders. The result: solid answers to nutritional questions and two dieticians now eating a lot of raw food.

If this topic interests you, just for fun on your travels I encourage you to visit raw-food restaurants and sample their amazing cuisine. In addition to Cafe Gratitude, mentioned previously, some restaurants I've enjoyed around the country include Raw Soul (www.rawsoul.com) and Pure Food and Wine (www.purefoodandwine.com), both in New York City; Grezzo (www.grezzorestaurant.com) in Boston; Karyn's Fresh Corner (www.karynraw.com) in Chicago; and in Santa Monica, Juliano's Raw (www.planetraw.com). And for connecting with raw-food folk from the comfort of your laptop, www.giveittomeraw.com is a lively and informative networking site.

Chapter 46, "KC, here I come"

Karma and consciousness are huge areas of study, but I have found some books that deal with them in a clear and nonacademic way. *Karma and*

Reincarnation: The Wisdom of Yogananda, volume 2, by Paramahansa Yogananda (Nevada City, CA: Crystal Clarity Publishers, 2007), is a short, understandable, and yet remarkably thorough introduction and explanation of karma from its source in the ancient Vedic tradition.

Chris Michaels, whose definition of consciousness I use in this essay, explains it further in his book *Your Soul's Assignment* (Kansas City, MO: Awakening World Enterprises, 2004). Chris is one of my mentors (I wrote the foreword for his book), and I have found that it is impossible to be around his words and his work without having a shift in consciousness.

Also cited here is Peace Pilgrim ("Live up to the highest light you have and more light will be given to you"). She was a twentieth-century mystic whose message is preserved in *Peace Pilgrim: Her Life and Work in Her Own Words,* edited by Friends of Peace Pilgrim (Santa Fe, NM: Ocean Tree Books, 1991).

Chapter 49, *"Love it. Then maybe leave it."*

One of the places I came to love a lot during my time in upstate New York was, as I mention in this essay, the Woodstock Farm Animal Sanctuary (www.woodstockfas.org). Visitors are welcome there and at the nearby Catskill Animal Sanctuary (www.casanctuary.org), in Saugerties, New York. The story of the Catskill shelter is told in *Where the Blind Horse Sings: Love and Healing at an Animal Sanctuary,* by Kathy Stevens (New York: Skyhorse Publishing, 2007). Other sanctuaries include Pigs, a Sanctuary (www.pigs.org), in Shepherdstown, West Virginia; Pigs Peace Sanctuary (www.pigspeace.org), in Stanwood, Washington; and the first and largest (it even features a bed and breakfast for guests), Farm Sanctuary (www.farmsanctuary.org), with locations in Watkins Glen, New York, and Orland, California. Farm Sanctuary cofounder Gene Baur chronicles its history and introduces some of the animals that live there in *Farm Sanctuary: Changing Hearts and Minds About Animals and Food* (New York: Touchstone, 2008).

To be in the company of friendly, curious cows, pigs, sheep, goats, turkeys, chickens, geese, and more (even the sanctuaries with the word *pigs* in their name have residents of other species), all rescued from very unsavory situations, is so uplifting. And for an urban or suburban kid, it's more fun than a theme park.

Permissions

Acknowledgments

I am deeply grateful to the dedicated people at HarperOne for their enthusiasm about this project, notably executive editor (and *my* editor, lucky me!) Gideon Weil and vice president and associate publisher Claudia Riemer Boutote, who first suggested that a tenth-anniversary sequel to *Creating a Charmed Life* was in order. Jan Baumer, Leslie Davisson, Carl Walesa, Lisa Zuniga, and a gifted team of people whose names I don't know yet are all responsible for this book. My literary agent, Linda Chester, has been a champion and sounding board throughout, as well as a role model for charmed living. And Karen Kelly, who acted as my freelance editor, breathed life into this project in a way I never could have done on my own.

My daughter, Adair Moran, provided a wealth of insight, from the proposal process to the completion of this book, and it was always a pleasure to meet her for "What do you think of this?" sessions and to vet which charmed-life principles would make the cut. It is also a continuous inspiration to me as a mom to see her pursuing a compassionate, creative, and charmed life of her own.

My great friend and "action partner" Sherry Boone was there with a phone call every morning, and she is responsible for several examples and anecdotes in this book. Other wonderful friends who have been in the cheering and inspiration section include Patti Breitman, Kay

Conway, Elizabeth Cutting, Olivia Fox, Rev. Evan Howard, Tom Martin, Consuelo Ribes, Rob Sanducci, Donna Vermeer, and Jennifer Wilkov. Insights for the book also came from Laura Allen, Alima, Alice Marie Bergman, Margery Barlow, Kay Fuller, Sharon Glassman, Janice Hunter, Lane Martin, Julie McGowan, Robert Morris, Mary Schmitt, Arlene Spool, Louann Stahl, Elaine Stefanowicz, and the late Fr. Paul Keenan.

Thanks to Nikia Dawkins, Gary Jaffe, and Xavier VanMeerbeek for making life easy; to the New Age Health Spa for inspiration and respite; and to Bread Alone in Woodstock, New York; Starbucks and Barnes & Noble in Kingston, New York; and Starbucks on Forty-ninth Street between Eighth and Ninth, in New York City: Thanks for the hospitality and electrical outlets.

I would like to thank Dottie Linscott and her Lucky Charms group, who inspired my use of that phrase for the action steps, and other readers of *Creating a Charmed Life* who contributed suggestions. They include Elvira Aletta, Cathy Allen, Ryan D. Andrews, Anne Bennett-Bready, Debbie Biggs, Janine Brown, Heather Burtner, Bonny Carmicino, Jeanette Blonigen Clancy, Linda Glover, Margaret Hanes, Tracie Hanson, Christine Hegstad, Dorothy P. Hill, Margaret "Taffy" Hill, James Igo, Beryl Kaighin, Danielle Kelly, Betty MacDonald, Michelle Martin, Sandy McMillrow, Julia Morley, Irma Negroni, Karen Nunes, Linda Parker, Starr Pellerin, Gayla Peppenfoht, Virginia Reese, Galina Rozetti, Gregg Sanderson, Ramona Seay, Karla Seidita, Kathy Stappenbeck, Marilyn Stroud, Patricia Williamson, Camille Wilson, Mariterese Woida, and Robert Yarnall.

Finally, to William: You were there for me every minute, every page, with everything from synonyms and computer help to your belief in me that keeps me going. I can't possibly thank you enough. And to my entire family and extended family: thank you with all my heart for giving me a focus and an anchor for my charmed life. ❧

250

About the Author

For more inspiration from Victoria Moran:

Blog: Read Victoria's daily blog, "Your Charmed Life," on BeliefNet.com, the Web's most comprehensive spirituality site: www.blog.beliefnet.com/yourcharmedlife.

Internet radio show: To listen to the monthly broadcast, "A Charmed Life," on Creative Health and Spirit Radio, tune in at noon Eastern time on the fourth Wednesday of every month, or access past programs via the station's archives. The URL for both live and archived programming is www.healthylife.net.

Newsletter: "The Charmed Monday Minute" goes out to subscribers on a monthly basis; there is no charge. Sign up at www.victoriamoran.com/contact.

Speaking for your business, church, or organization: Victoria's presentations are content-rich, inspiring, funny, and filled with touching and humorous stories your audience won't soon forget. View her speaker demo at www.victoriamoran.com, and read more about her keynotes and workshops on the

speaker page of the site. You can then book her directly
or be referred to a speakers' bureau that represents her.

Charm-your-life coaching: Victoria is a certified life coach
specializing in spiritual-life coaching, helping you tap the
wisdom already inside you to create greater fulfillment,
reach your goals, and bring your dreams to fruition. For
more information, see www.victoriamoran.com/coaching.

Web site: To learn more about this author, her other books,
and when she'll be speaking in your area, please visit
www.victoriamoran.com.